ORIENTAL LACQUER

Oscar Luzzato-Bilitz

ORIENTAL LACQUER

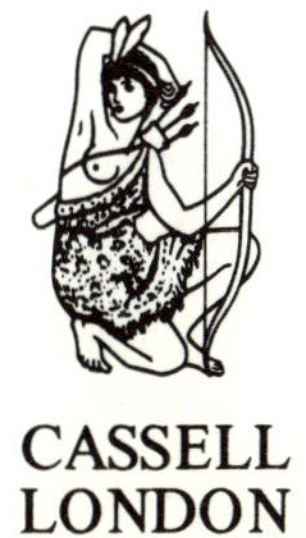

CASSELL
LONDON

Cassell Publishers Limited
Artillery House, Artillery Row
London SW1P 1RT

Translated by Pauline L. Phillips from the Italian original
Lacche Orientali

© Gruppo Editoriale Fabbri, Bompiani, Sonzogno, Etas S.p.A., Milan 1966, 1984

This edition 1988

All rights reserved. This book is protected by copyright. No part of it may be reproduced, stored in a retrieval system, or transmitted in any form or by any means, electronic, mechanical, photocopying or otherwise, without written permission from the Publishers.

British Library Cataloguing in Publication Data
Luzzato-Bilitz, Oscar
Oriental lacquer. — (Cassell's styles in art).
1. Asian lacquer ware
I. Title II. Lacche Orientali. *English*
745.7'3'0951

ISBN 0-304-32184-2

Printed in Italy by Gruppo Editoriale Fabbri S.p.A., Milan

CONTENTS

	Page
Origins and Techniques	7
Ancient Chinese Lacquers	20
Japanese Lacquers	98
List of Illustrations	133

ORIGINS AND TECHNIQUES

Oriental lacquers were brought to Europe at the beginning of the 17th century, first by the Portuguese and soon afterwards by the Dutch. About this time Venetian and Genoese furniture-makers were attempting to make furniture with the brilliantly-coloured and painted varnishing that was to become so fashionable in the 18th century. The superiority of Chinese lacquers over European varnishes was obvious, and many attempts were made to imitate them. The influence of Chinese lacquer on furniture-making was felt throughout the 18th and in part of the 19th century. Chinese porcelain was also imported into Europe in large quantities. Its figurative decoration, typical of the period, was quite new to most Westerners, and in Venice and England gave rise to the styles known as Venetian lacquered *chinoiseries* and Chippendale Chinese.

Towards the end of the 18th century, Chinese lacquer work was showing a marked decline, though in any case objects made for export to the 'Western barbarian lands' were not of the best quality. At the same time, exquisitely-made Japanese lacquered works, usually small in size and with a foundation of gold, appeared on the European market. Understandably enough, Europeans came to believe that the art must have been Japanese in origin; and the English even coined the curious term 'japanning'—still sometimes used today—to describe lacquer-work. For a long time the Japanese did indeed claim to have been its inventors. This assertion was given credibility by the fact that lacquering was regarded in China as a mere craft or, at best, a minor art-form; the only recognised arts, whose most famous exponents had been recorded and commented upon in all periods, were calligraphy, painting, poetry and, to some extent, music. Lacquering had always been admired, but there were few literary allusions to its development or its ancient exponents. In Japan, on the other hand, the chronicles recorded an uninterrupted series of 'masters of lacquer', the first of whom was supposed to have been Mitsumi-no-Sukunè, who lived at the court of the Emperor Koan Tennō towards the end of the 4th century BC. The word 'Tennō' forms part of the name of all Japanese Emperors, and may be translated as 'descended from Heaven'; it signifies the divine origin of the imperial house which reigned without interruption for about twenty-six centuries.

The accounts given in ancient Chinese texts of the use of lacquer from remote antiquity were rejected by the Japanese as apocryphal; and until a few decades ago there were no archaeological discoveries that supported the texts. Today, in the light of research and excavations—though these are far from complete—it is clear that lacquer was used in China some considerable time before the hypothetical Mitsumi-no-Sukunè. This adds weight to the contention that Japan, most of whose art derives from China, is also indebted to her for the technique of working in lacquer.

For a long time, the hypothesis that the Japanese invented lacquer techniques independently seemed supported by the maritime isolation of Japan. Ancient Chinese vessels were extremely frail, and suitable only for crossing rivers, not for facing the open sea, let alone the Yellow Sea, which is often swept by terrible storms. Many Japanese also maintained that their sailors had brought back objects and goods from raids on the coasts of China; and that this accounted for the Chinese influence apparent in many Japanese art-forms. According to this theory, the Japanese succeeded in reproducing and improving upon Chinese work without tuition.

Such an account is not very convincing. Japanese history begins only in 660 BC, that is, late in the Chou period, when China already had more than a thousand years of recorded history behind her. And even this beginning is legendary: in concrete historical terms Japan does not go back beyond the Christian era. For this reason Chinese emigration into Japan before the Christian era is much more likely. The most important reference in the ancient chronicles is still unsupported, though the persistence of the story over the centuries suggests that it has some foundation in fact. The Emperor Wu Ti the Great (141-87 BC), of the Han dynasty, became a fervent Taoist. After he had extended his kingdom as far as the Pamirs and given peace to the whole of China, he decided to try to discover and colonise the Isle of the Blessed. In the Taoist creed this is a kind of earthly paradise which was then believed to lie in the direction of the rising sun. At the end of the 2nd century BC, Wu Ti is said to have ordered an expedition of a hundred vessels or so to carry to the island some 500 young men and women, and a retinue of soldiers, workmen and slaves. If the expedition (an enormous one for the period) did take place, it in all probability set sail from the mouth of the Yangtse-kiang, close to present-day Nanking. The outcome is not recorded. Did any of those frail junks in fact land in Japan, or were they all destroyed in a storm? The crossing of the Yellow Sea in little wooden sailing boats with woven straw sails was undoubtedly a desperate undertaking.

In any event, it is certain that there had already been periodic Chinese migrations to Japan by another route: from Korea. This corner of Asia projects into the sea towards the Japanese archipelago, and its ethnic nucleus was probably formed by the nomadic tribes of Manchuria who came down from the north. But the whole of Northern and Central Korea was colonised by the Chinese some time before the birth of Christ. Chinese chronicles relate that in 1122 BC (1027 BC, according to modern historians) Prince Fa defeated the former Chinese sovereign Yin, and killed him; he became the first emperor of the Chou dynasty. The former sovereign's uncle, Prince Ch'i Tzu, fled to Korea with 5000 followers; there he founded the kingdom of Chao-hsien. (The whole of Korea was later known by this Chinese name.) A little later, King Wu (the title assumed by Prince Fa) recognised the sovereignty of Ch'i Tzu, who became the nominal vassal of the Chou emperor; in return he was guaranteed military assistance in time of need. Presumably the new Chinese monarch of Korea brought with him the already highly-developed culture of his native land.

Ch'i Tzu's successors reigned undisturbed for about nine centuries, extending their territories to include the whole of north-western Korea and also perhaps occupying part of southern Manchuria. The forty-first and last descendant of Ch'i Tzu was deposed in 193 BC by a Chinese mercenary captain called Wei Man. Wei Man was a skilful politician, and extended the boundaries of his kingdom considerably; but his immediate successor, Yu Ch'u, was rash enough to challenge the Han Empire at the height of its power, refusing to pay the customary tributes. In 109 BC – and from this point the dates are unquestionable – three mighty armies, sent by the Chinese Emperor, Wu Ti, laid siege to the capital of the Sino-Korean kingdom, which now included all the western part of the northern and central provinces of the peninsula (Liao-tung and Lolang). In the following year, Yu Ch'u was forced by his own officials to give in, and the Han Emperor set up four military colonies in Korea, occupying almost the entire land except the eastern coast and the southern cape; Korea became completely Chinese (108 BC). Throughout the turbulent 'Warring States' period (481-221 BC) and the series of wars and domestic struggles in Korea itself, Chinese craftsmen undoubtedly emigrated to Korea, and later Japan, in search of settled conditions and good pay. The Japanese themselves, who were able to reach the southern tip of Korea without very much difficulty, sent embassies in search of workers. It seems, therefore, that it was either the Chinese or the Koreans who first introduced and taught their arts in Japan.

The abundance of recent finds of lacquer objects in the area of Lolang, dating from the 4th century BC to the 2nd century AD, will be discussed in more detail later on. It is mentioned here because it implies that there was a fully developed and varied manufacture of lacquer in Korea, and that the tree from which the resin was extracted was indigenous to the place. Possibly, then, the Chinese introduced into Japan the first cuttings or seeds which led to the creation of plantations of *Rhus vernicifera*.

The origin and preparation of the raw material are the same everywhere. The *lac* (sap) or resin of the *Rhus vernicifera* is the natural source of lacquer. This tree grows wild in all parts of China, particularly on the high plateaux above the 6500-7000 foot line; in ancient times it must also have flourished in the vast region of the central plain, where it was later replaced by the cereals needed to feed a growing population. A large number of works have recently been found in the Ch'ang Sha area in Hunan province, in tombs dating from the late Chou to the succeeding Han dynasty. This is a sure indication that the raw material – the trees – were to be found *in situ*.

The technique of extracting the resin has not changed over the centuries and is similar to that used to extract rubber. When the tree is about eight to ten years old, a horizontal slash is made in the bark and a small copper cup is tied under the incision to catch the resin as it oozes out. Initially this appears as a whitish, transparent sap which thickens and becomes darker in contact with the air until it becomes blackish. This transformation is analogous to that of the latex of the *Hevea* (rubber tree) or the poppy which yields raw opium. By contrast with rubber, which has to be shaped into rounded balls and then smoke-cured, lacquer has to be submitted to prolonged boiling, skimming and filtering through a hempen cloth, in order to remove earth and vegetable impurities. It is then ready for use.

If a perfect result is to be obtained (and one was always sought in ancient China and Japan), the technique of application must be both delicate and slow. To achieve brilliance and toughness, innumerable layers of lacquer must be applied thinly one upon another. Each lightly-applied coat must be allowed to harden and dry before the operation is repeated. The work requires patience and time because the drying process cannot be hurried and must take place in a damp atmosphere; otherwise the lacquer may become fragile and flake off. For this repetitive operation, many Chinese still use the ingenious vapour-bath invented many centuries ago. Once it is dry, each layer of lacquer is smoothed by hand with fine charcoal dust. Finally, when the lacquering is judged to be of the right thickness, the surface is levelled again, this time with horn ash. This is of course the classic technique employed by ancient Chinese artists for more than two thousand years: it is doubtful whether it is kept up today. Certain deeply incised lacquers may have been given from 200 to 300 coats, which makes it easy to understand why this art has remained the prerogative of the patient oriental.

This lengthy and difficult process, so summarily dealt with here, is what may be called the craft part. The 'art'–that is, the decoration of a lacquered object –may be carried out with a brush, using lacquer with added pigment, much as a painter creates a picture; or the object may be enriched with inlays of gold or silver in imitation of ancient metal-inlaid ritual bronzes. Although it became fashionable only from the 17th century, the use of inlaid mother-of-pearl or ivory is of very ancient origin, and it is for this type of lacquer that the French coined the name '*laque burgautée*'. Finally, very thick lacquer, made by applying many successive layers, may be incised with geometric, floral or figural designs.

Most lacquer work is applied upon a framework. For large works, especially in China, this was always made of soft, light wood. Besides being decorative, lacquering serves as a protection against damp and weather. The ancient process was as follows. The wood was shaped or carved into the required form; if it was flat (to make panels or furniture), it was usually reduced to fine panels skilfully luted and stuck together; if it was to serve for a sculpture of some size, several pieces were carved separately and then fitted together with some kind of wooden peg. (Screws and nails came into use in China only during the 19th century.) Once the framework was finished, a hempen or China grass cloth was fixed on it and a kind of chalky dressing applied to it with a brush or spatula. The dressing contained an ingredient which gave it a certain hardness once it was completely dry; this ingredient may have been the inferior quality lacquer which was (as old records indicate) originally used.

When all these operations had been completed, the actual lacquering took place. When the work was finished and the lacquer perfectly dry and hard, it was rubbed down by hand with fine ash. For small objects, such as cups or small boxes, the frame was very often simply hemp, and a different method was used. If the object to be made consisted of flat surfaces, a cloth was stretched on a wooden model or mould and stiffened by a priming of lacquer; the model was then removed and the lacquering of the other parts could proceed. A cloth could only be stretched over a curved surface by sticking it on; so in this case the model was made of crude clay which was scraped away after the external lacquering.

For sculptures of medium size, a mixture of mud, ashes and fibre was sometimes used instead of a wooden core, and some kind of vegetable drying oil was probably added. The process used for lacquering was the same, except that there was no intermediary cloth: the dressing was smeared directly on to the surface of the sculpture, which (when the dressing had dried) had the appearance and durability of cemented stucco. The making of such quasi-stucco in China is a very ancient practice, going as far back as the Six Dynasties period (265-589); but it appears that this type of statuary, probably of Gupta origin, would not have been lacquered prior to the 10th and 11th centuries. The specimen illustrated here (plate 9), a Kuan Yin (Bodhisattva of Compassion), is about 27½ inches high, quite heavy, and completely covered in gold lacquer in a perfect state of preservation; it may be dated to the 14th century.

The 'dry lacquer' technique, which was comparatively little used in China (except for small objects), consists in lacquering without a rigid framework. Direct casting of the lacquer was also used to make statuettes. First a model was made in dry clay and a mould obtained from it. Then lacquer was cast in the two halves of the mould; it had to be sufficiently thick for it to be pressed into the most intricate parts of the mould with a wet finger. Once they had dried and hardened in the air, the casts were detached and the two halves bonded with liquid lacquer. Finally the lacquer was smoothed over to hide the join.

In Japan, dry lacquering was also used in the 9th

to 11th centuries for large statues, especially for those that had to be light enough to be carried in processions. The process was substantially the same as that which has already been briefly dealt with in mentioning the core-less Chinese boxes. For statues, the artist modelled the clay in great detail, and the structure was supported inside by a bamboo frame. When the sections were dry, they were assembled and covered with a dressing that set hard, allowing the finishing touches to be applied; then the whole thing was thickly lacquered. When the lacquer had hardened, the clay and bamboo supports were cautiously removed, leaving a hollow shell which was made quite strong by the lacquering it had received. Of course, the lacquer had to be smoothed by hand-rubbing with charcoal dust before the statue was hollowed out. It appears that the Japanese did their lacquering on the banks of a river, thus obtaining the dampness necessary for a slow hardening; this made for greater durability. If the interior of the statue was wholly of wood, it was not of course possible to hollow it out completely. However, both the Chinese and Japanese contrived to remove all useless parts at a late stage in the process, perhaps to avoid eventual warping of the wood through heat or humidity. This meant that they were left with a hole which had to be closed up again with a square wedge. If you open this kind of chamber in the back of ancient statues, almost all of which represent Buddha, you may easily find the remains of dried flowers, and rolls of paper or silk with long inscriptions on them. These inscriptions are sometimes dedicatory – when they nearly always carry a date or some other indication which makes it possible to establish when the work was made – and sometimes supplicatory, imploring a favour of the divinity represented. No examples of statues portraying real historical characters have been found in China; only generalised representations of the Buddhist pantheon.

Known examples of incised lacquer date back no further than the Mongol Yuan dynasty (1280-1368), although some ancient texts say that they originated much earlier. Whatever the truth, it may safely be said that incised lacquer did not come into normal production until that period. Until the 19th century, the required thickness of lacquer was obtained by applying anything up to 300 successive coats, which was expensive as well as laborious. Today it is obtained simply by casting, and, for the sake of economy, the material used almost always contains ochre, oils and other cheap substances. Modern lacquers are no longer works of art; they are more in the nature of bazaar items. A final example of the loving care displayed by the old Chinese craftsman: he often laid on alternate layers of different coloured lacquers so that, when the piece was incised, a background of contrasting colour emerged beneath the decoration.

ANCIENT CHINESE LACQUERS

A monumental history of China, from the remotest antiquity until the 1st century BC, was written at the command of the Han Emperor Wu Ti. It relates that Shun, the last of the Five Sages (according to tradition he reigned from 2255 to 2205 BC), taught his people to use the natural sap of a tree to protect and beautify the wood used to construct their homes.

A more precise reference to the use of lacquer is contained in a book attributable to the 9th century BC. It is the first text on stringed musical instruments, written for Li Wang (861-841 BC), tenth of the Western Chou rulers. He was a feeble ruler, and in 841 BC—the first date in Chinese history which is accepted as exact—one of his rebellious generals compelled him to abandon the throne and flee. He was, however, a great lover of the arts, especially music. The text describes lutes and similar musical instruments of the time, which were elegantly decorated with coloured lacquer. There are later copies of other books purporting to have been written during the Chou period; but their datings are not always recognised as authentic. They contain references to the use of lacquer to decorate bows, cross-bows, carts, furniture and other objects. To my mind, this literary evidence is too easily rejected as apocryphal by modern scholars; for a relatively recent series of excavations of various Shang-

Yin capitals (16th-11th centuries BC) has given fairly conclusive proof that lacquer was in use.

The only objects recovered from these tombs thirty to thirty-five centuries old were, of course, those made from practically indestructible materials such as bronze or pottery. In some tombs, however, the earth still bears the outlines of the carts and other wooden objects placed there; and among their crumbled remains have been found fragments of reddish pigment, the remains of lacquer. It should be remembered that in this remote period lacquer was used more as a means of preserving wood than for decorative purposes. The first pigment used for colouring was probably cinnabar, which occurs naturally in all parts of China; there are references in the oldest chronicles to the red pillars which embellished the halls of mythical sovereigns' palaces. It has been proved that, during the 'feudal' Chou dynasty (1122-256 BC, according to official accounts), lacquer objects were used as gifts or tribute; they were sent not only by vassals to their lord, but also to the rulers of neighbouring states. Proof positive of this has been given by archaeological discoveries in Manchuria, Turkestan and Annam, and by infrequent but widely-scattered finds of lacquered objects (or fragments) in localities far from central China. These indicate that the art had already attained a high level of development.

Two digs carried out thirty years ago have provided information which made possible a comparative study of the art of lacquer in China between the 4th century BC and the 2nd century AD. One was made in the area south of the middle reaches of the Yangtsekiang; the other in Korea. At Ch'ang Sha (Hunan province), the ancient capital of the state of Ch'u, one of the great vassal states of the Chou kingdom, there are tombs dating from the 4th century BC to the 1st century AD. An enormous number of painted lacquer objects have been found in them, mostly in an excellent state of preservation—implying that the technique was highly developed. Most of them are small objects for daily use in a sophisticated society: toilet boxes, cylindrical brushpots, drinking-cups and bowls, trays and so on. The boxes, like the cups, are round or oval; the lacquer on the sides and lids is painted, while the lacquer on the bottom is almost always plain black. All the decoration is figurative: the trays and boxes often carry delicate and graceful family scenes portraying ladies. Other examples, by contrast, have processions of horsemen very similar in style to those found on painted tiles in Han tombs, and probably date from the same period. The commonest design in the oldest works, however, is a geometric and abstract stylisation of dragons or parts of dragons with spirals and whorls; they closely resemble pre-Han bronzes in style.

The lacquered wood sculpture found in the necropolis on the outskirts of Ch'ang Sha differs completely from the traditional style—so much so that for a time there was speculation about possible foreign influences. The best-known sculpture (plate 1) is an object of uncertain purpose consisting of two birds with extremely long, slender necks and disproportionately tiny bodies; they stand back to back on a base formed by the intertwined bodies of two serpents. The bodies of the birds, like those of the serpents, are decorated with polychrome lacquer in a design of feathers and scales in black and red with a few touches of yellow. The birds' breasts and the dorsal band on the snakes, on the other hand, have a stylised geometric decoration—triangles and squares with small internal spirals—in the classic style of the 'Warring States' period (481-256 BC). In modern studies the birds are usually said to be cranes (one of the creatures sacred to the Taoists), and some orientalists claim that the piece is a symbolic representation of the triumph of spirituality over earthly cunning. It seems to me, however, that the shape is more like that of the heron or ibis in Indo-Chinese sculpture from Burma or Annam. This work, at present in the Cleveland Museum of Art, is held to date from the 4th century BC, a dating that seems to be correct.

Another lacquered wood sculpture, now in the British Museum, was also found in a tomb at Ch'ang Sha, and probably dates from the same period. At first sight it appears even less Chinese in style. It represents a grotesque human head with an elongated tongue hanging out of its mouth and stag's horns growing from the top of its head. The discovery of similar works in southern Honan and Shensi—the centre, so to speak, of Chinese civilisation—has disposed of the theory of foreign influence. It seems to me that such pieces may be a primitive form of the terrifying terracotta figures found in tombs of the period from the immediate post-Han era to the end of the T'ang dynasty. These statuettes were at first zoomorphic, shaped like an imaginary animal with a long dorsal ridge, and have frequently been found in the tombs of the Six Dynasties (AD 265-589). Later, the figures evolved into hybrid shapes, with bodies of imaginary animals and human heads of fearsome aspect. Laufer identifies these as Yama, the God of Death, who in the T'ang period became Lokapala, the Guardian of the Tombs; they are generally regarded as defenders of the peace of the dead. There was, however, a Chinese belief, widespread for thousands of years, that the body had a multiplicity of souls or spirits, only the highest of which quitted it at the time of death; the other, 'terrestrial' ones remained there for some time. They had to be symbolically fed with offerings and then, by means of special purification ceremonies, gradually induced to withdraw. In view of this, the function of the imaginary beings represented by these statuettes is likely to have been that of keeping watch on the earth-bound spirits, preventing them from leaving the tomb and troubling the relatives of the dead man.

The symbolism of the horns in the work in the British Museum, as in similar works later found in other regions of China, seems to be connected with the totemic cult common to many tribes of ancient Siberia. The shamans of the northern regions wore a kind of diadem made from the horns of reindeer or stags on their heads; it symbolised their ability to move freely and rapidly between the real and spirit worlds. One of their tasks was to accompany the souls of the dead to their eternal resting place.

The most sensational discovery, however, took place in about 1931-1932 in Korea, and was the work of Japanese archaeologists. In the burial area of Lolang, the ancient kingdom of the Chinese Ch'i Tzu in west-central Korea, countless lacquered objects were found dating from the 3rd century BC to the 2nd century AD. The most important tomb—for the quality rather than the number of finds—was made famous by one particular work; and as a result it is always called 'the Tomb of the Painted Basket'. The basket, now in the museum at Seoul, belonged to a rich Chinese nobleman and was buried with him towards the end of the 1st century AD. It has an ornamental band of flowering vine tendrils with a central decoration of a line of seated male figures; these are painted in lacquer of vivid hues—reds, whites, yellows and greens—and portrayed with a lively and brilliant realism. All the other objects found in the tomb (a casket, drinking-cups, toilet boxes, trays and so on) were decorated with a much simpler design in yellow and red on a background of black lacquer; the style, oddly enough, appears to be pre-Han. In fact this decoration consists essentially of spirals and whorls of stylised dragons, motifs which belong to the end of the Chou period; yet the abundance of works with similar decoration precludes the hypothesis that the objects were buried at an earlier date.

The chronicles of the Han dynasty (206 BC-AD 220) were faithfully transcribed over the centuries, almost up to modern times. In them, and in the work on Chinese art partly translated by Bushell, reference is made to the interest shown by the Emperor Wu Ti in lacquer work. It was undoubtedly Wu Ti or his immediate successor who issued a decree placing the craft under the direct patronage of the Emperor. Towards the beginning of the Christian era, workshops were set up at the command of the Emperor; there an official overseer, backed up by a corps of guards, supervised the manufacture of objects to be used at court or sent to important Chinese functionaries or foreign princes. The chronicles of the Han dynasty record only three of these workshops, in Szechwan,

Honan and Kiangsu provinces respectively; but there must have been more, probably about ten. Perhaps the three workshops mentioned produced exclusively for the Emperor, which would account for the omission of the others.

A magnificent lacquered drinking-vessel with two flanged handles (British Museum, plate 5) was found in a tomb in the old capital of Lolang. It carries a date which corresponds to 44 BC; that is, during the period when Lolang was a Chinese possession. It is certainly not Korean work, as the long inscription on it confirms: it records that the bowl was given to a high functionary as a supreme mark of recognition of his services. The Emperor Yuan Ti (48-33 BC) was then on the throne of China, and it was he who ordered the overseer of the western workshop in Szechwan to send it to the functionary. The literal translation of this inscription is as follows: 'Fourth year Yuan Ti. Shru Command [in Szechwan]. Western workshop. Imperial drinking-cup of painted lacquered wood. Gilded handles. Capacity 1 *sheng* and 16 *yueh* [liquid measures]. First work, Yi [name of the carpenter who made the thin wood framework]. Preparation of lacquer, Li [workman whose task was to put the dressed cloth covering on the wood]. General lacquering, Tang. Gilding of handles, Ku. Painting, Ting. Incising, Feng. Polishing, Ping. Responsible for production, Tsung Tsao. Guard Commander of the workshop, Chang. Manager, Liang. Overseer, Pao Chou.' The bare list of names reveals the high degree of specialisation and strict supervision of work in the Imperial workshops.

The marked and dated works which have come to light in Chinese and Korean tombs were all made in the official workshops. It is clear that the inscription was the last of many operations, each of which was entrusted to a specialist and carried out under bureaucratic control in accordance with strict instructions. Personal and artistic initiative on the part of the craftsman was precluded; indeed it is probable that approved sketches or designs were sent to the workshop from some artistic centre near the court. Bureaucratic control and the kind of work ordered fostered conservatism; and this provides a convincing reason why lacquers executed in the Han period should display the same antiquated style of decoration as bronze mirrors of the Chou period (triangles and whorls with dragons and other animals so stylised as to be practically unrecognisable). There was much artistic activity in Ch'ang Sha (Hunan province) throughout the Han period, though tombs dating from the end of the period have not yielded the same abundance and variety of lacquered objects as those from the centuries immediately preceding it. Generally speaking, finds have been limited to bows, cross-bows and tables; there are no traces of the fantastic and terrifying figures found in tombs of the 3rd and 4th centuries BC.

In the winter of the year AD 8, the usurper Wang Mang dethroned the last ruler of the direct Han line; but in AD 25 a collateral branch of the dynasty took power. During this second Han dynasty (25-220), the capital was moved further east, to Loyang. This was further from the principal Imperial workshops, and it is perhaps for this reason that they declined. The decline was not of course immediate; in fact the first result of diminished Imperial control may have been a more varied artistic production. There is, for example, a splendid tray, made in the Shu workshop in the west, which is decorated quite differently from the traditional manner of the late Chou period. It carries a circular band of tiny stags around the figure of a woman, probably the mythical Hsi Wang Mu (the 'Queen of the West'). The tray was discovered in 1931 by two Japanese archaeologists, Koizumi and Sana, in the tomb of a Chinese functionary called Wang Kuang; according to the incised tablet which was also found there, he was buried in AD 69. Simultaneously with the gradual disappearance of inscribed lacquer works from the workshops under direct Imperial control, there was a renaissance of individual lacquer work, as recent archaeological discoveries have demonstrated. New designs, no longer geometrically stylised but with a greater wealth and variety of figurative decoration, make it clear that a large number of important artists were active in the late Han period; unfortunately, we know nothing about them. Variations of decorative style in lacquer work between the 5th or 4th centuries BC and the end of the Han dynasty are most strikingly exemplified in the continuous and abundant production unearthed in the Lolang area.

The famous 'Tomb of the Painted Basket', which dates from the 1st or 2nd century AD, yielded many objects in addition to the basket described earlier. These were catalogued and illustrated in a work published in Japanese (Tokyo, 1934) and partly translated into French by Haguenauer. It briefly mentions a splendid lacquered table-top with a red background and decoration in gold, silver, and a range of yellows, blacks and greens. It contains a wealth of designs: sinuous dragons (a distant heritage of the styles of the 'Warring States'), as well as young stags *couchants* and small running figures which are clearly Han. (They are also found on the many grey incised ceramic tiles which were originally part of the walls of 1st- and 2nd-century burial chambers.) Another discovery was a magnificent cylinder which probably contained an important document; it has fine red decoration on a background of black lacquer.

By way of a summary, it may be said that the tumult of the 'Warring States' period found expression in an art with sinuous curves and imaginary snake-like creatures which intertwine and curl upon themselves as if in continuous, convulsive movement; whereas the *Pax Sinica* of the four centuries of Han domination were characterised by a gradual return to tranquillity, with freer rhythms and more figurative motifs.

During the 1st century AD, the number of gifts and tributes leaving the Imperial workshops seems to have been reduced, doubtless because the court was forced to economise after the interregnum between AD 9 and AD 25. The large number of lacquer objects found in Korea and dating from later than the 1st century must therefore have been largely of local manufacture; yet in style and technique they are identical with Imperial work. Their makers must have been Chinese, some of them probably from the Imperial workshops (which were almost certainly closed by the end of the 1st century). An exceptional work now in the British Museum (plate 3) seems to belong to this period. It is a round box with a convex lid about 4 inches in diameter, lacquered on cloth except for the base, which has a thin wooden disc as its frame. The outside has a brown background with a very delicate red decoration of curved lines and fanciful creatures. There is a quatrefoil silver inlay in the centre of the lid; other inlays, representing running animals and a mounted archer releasing an arrow, are also in silver but have largely worn away. The inside is of plain vermilion lacquer. Circular bands on the rim of the lid and the sides contain the geometric motifs—circles, triangles and whorls—found on contemporary bronze mirrors.

During the Han period, sculpture and ceramics became heavy, ponderous and sober; lacquering, by contrast, was evolving with a richness and variety of design which could only have been created by great artists, albeit unknown and unsung. Over the whole period between the two great dynasties, the Han and the T'ang (which began in 618), lacquer was apparently neglected, in spite of the high level it had reached in the preceding centuries. This is all the more strange in that, although this, the era of the Six Dynasties, was tumultuous, it cannot be said that art in general fell into decline. During the reign of the Northern Wei (386-536), in fact, statue sculpture attained an artistic level which in certain respects has never been surpassed; and in the state of Yu (Chekiang) glazed ceramics of outstanding beauty were created.

As far as the flourishing Chinese lacquer manufacture in Korea is concerned, it must be remembered that in 313 China split into numerous states, and lost

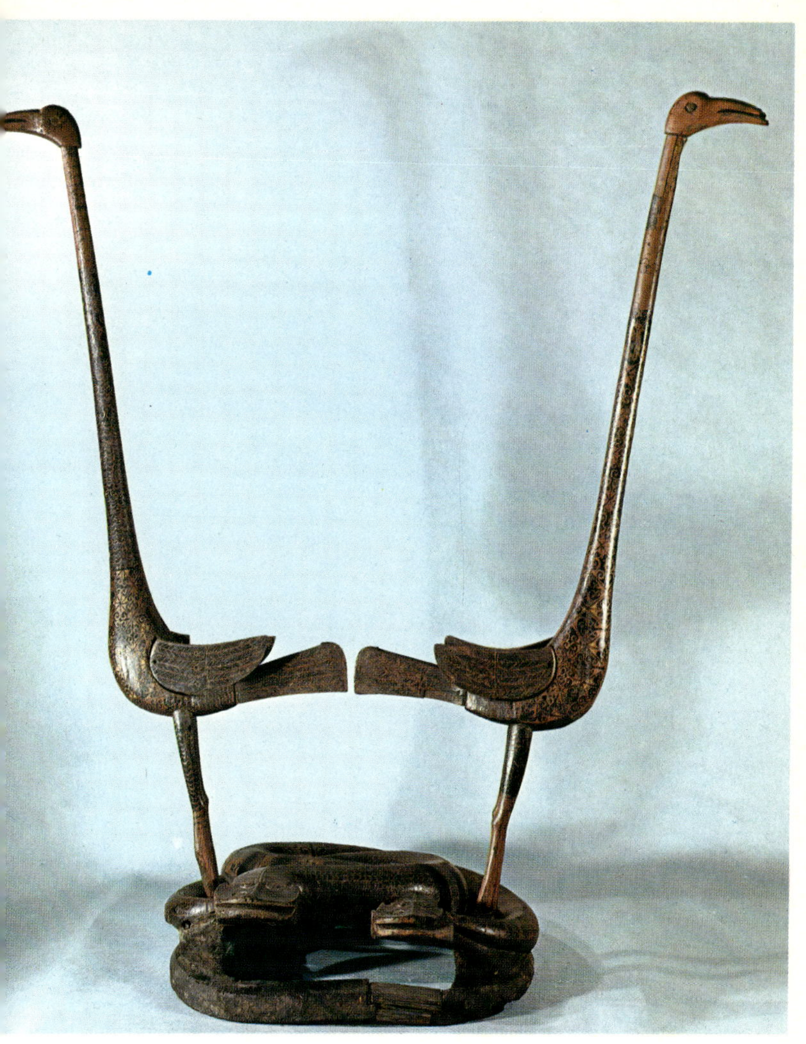

1. Decorative object. 4th-3rd century BC. J.H. Wade Fund, Cleveland Museum of Art, Cleveland.

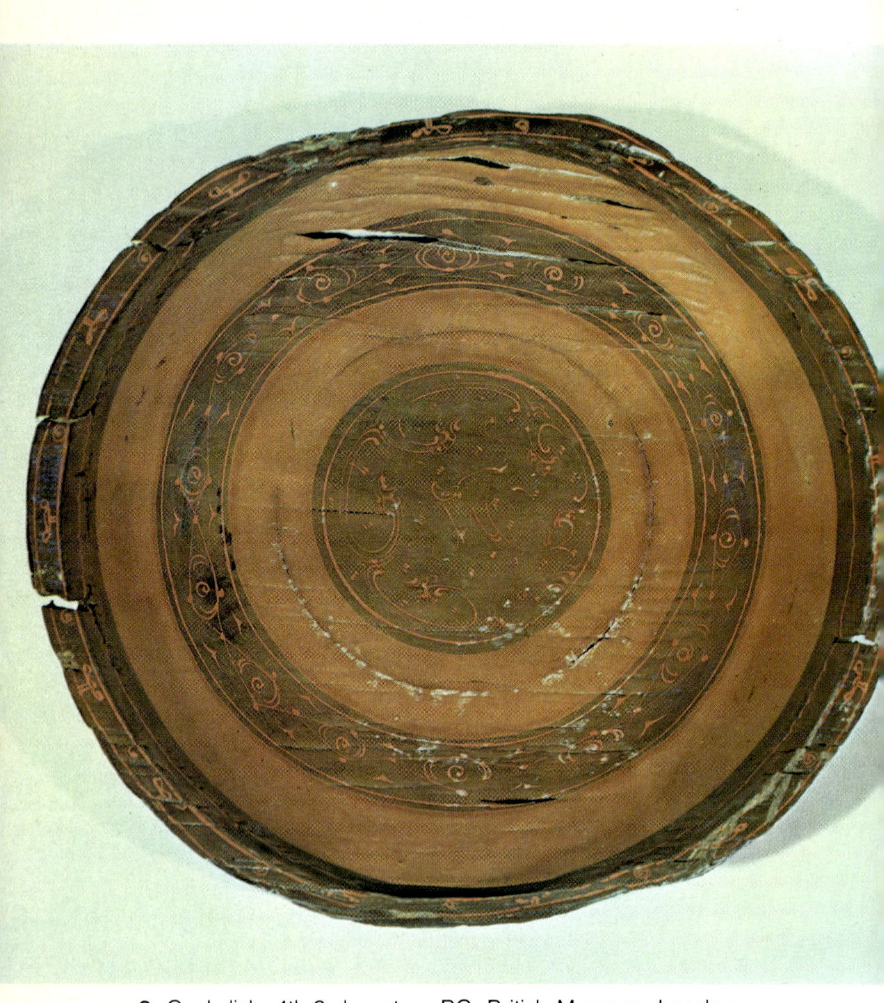

2. Oval dish. 4th-3rd century BC. British Museum, London.

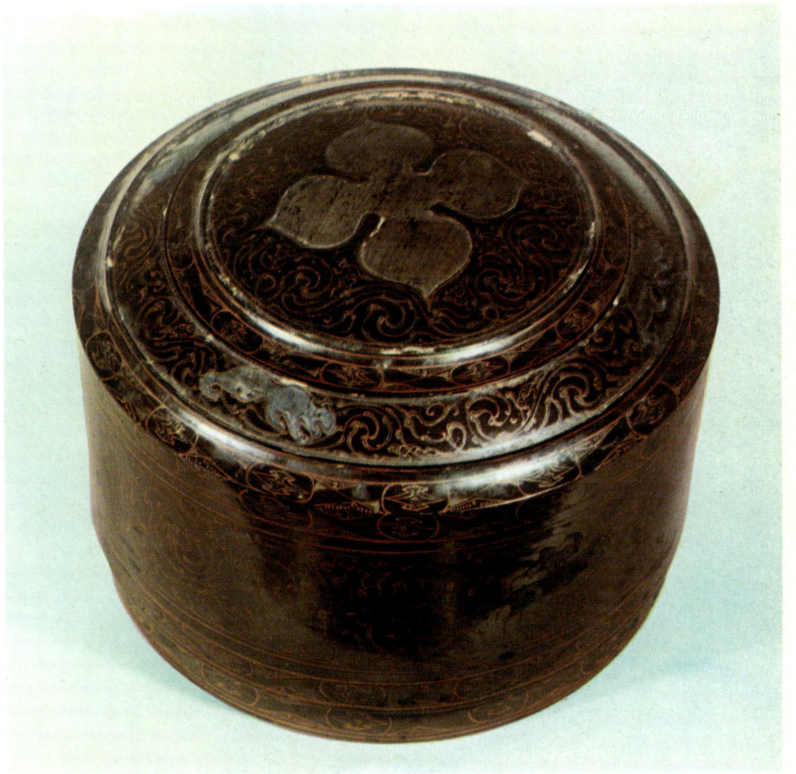

3. Round box for powder or rouge. 1st century AD. British Museum, London.

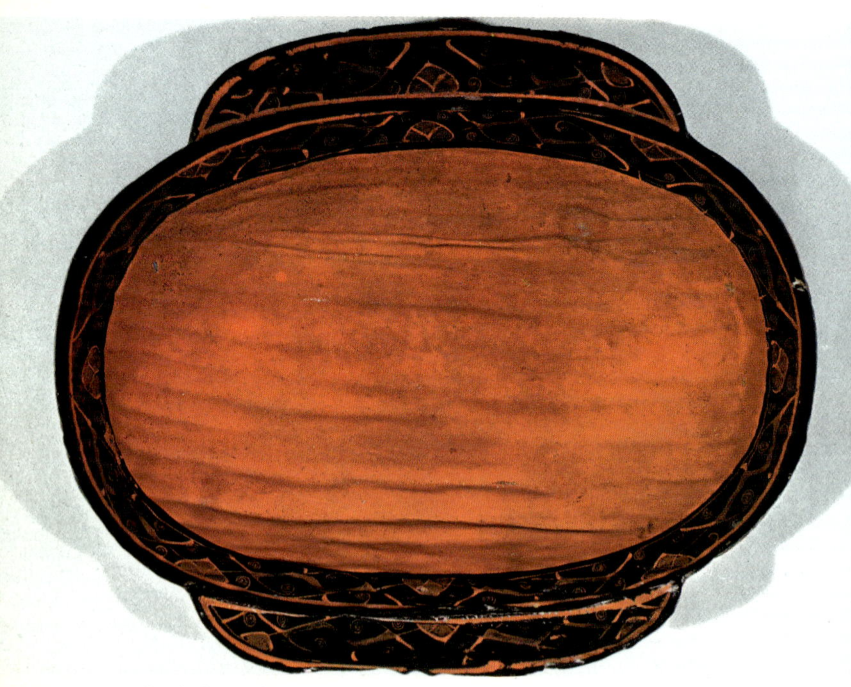

4. Oval dish with side flanges. 4th-3rd century BC. British Museum, London.

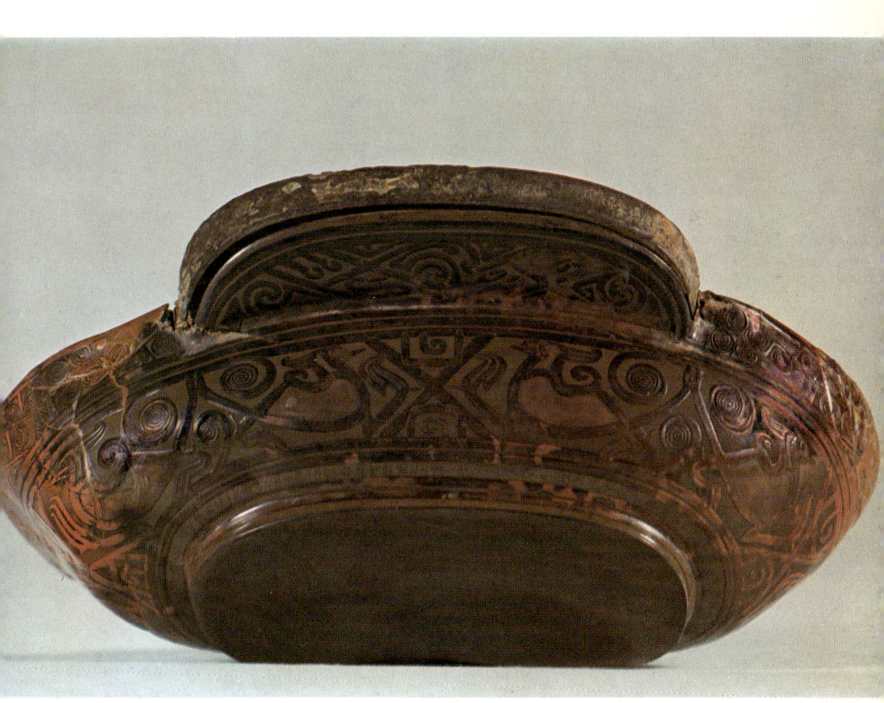

5. Oval bowl with two flanged handles. 1st century BC. British Museum, London.

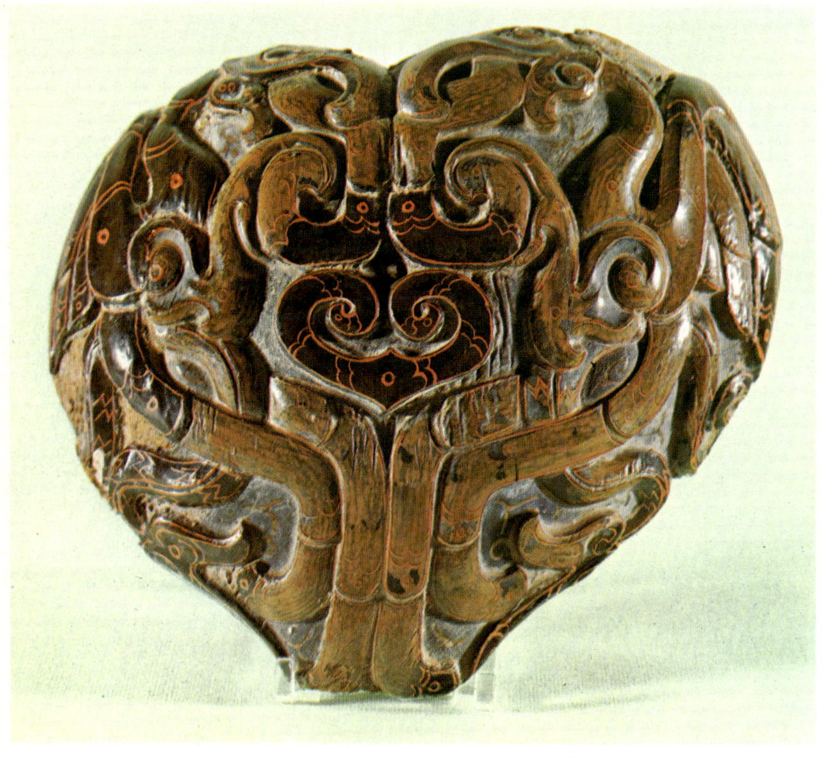

6. Decorative antefix. 3rd-6th century. Musée Guimet, Paris.

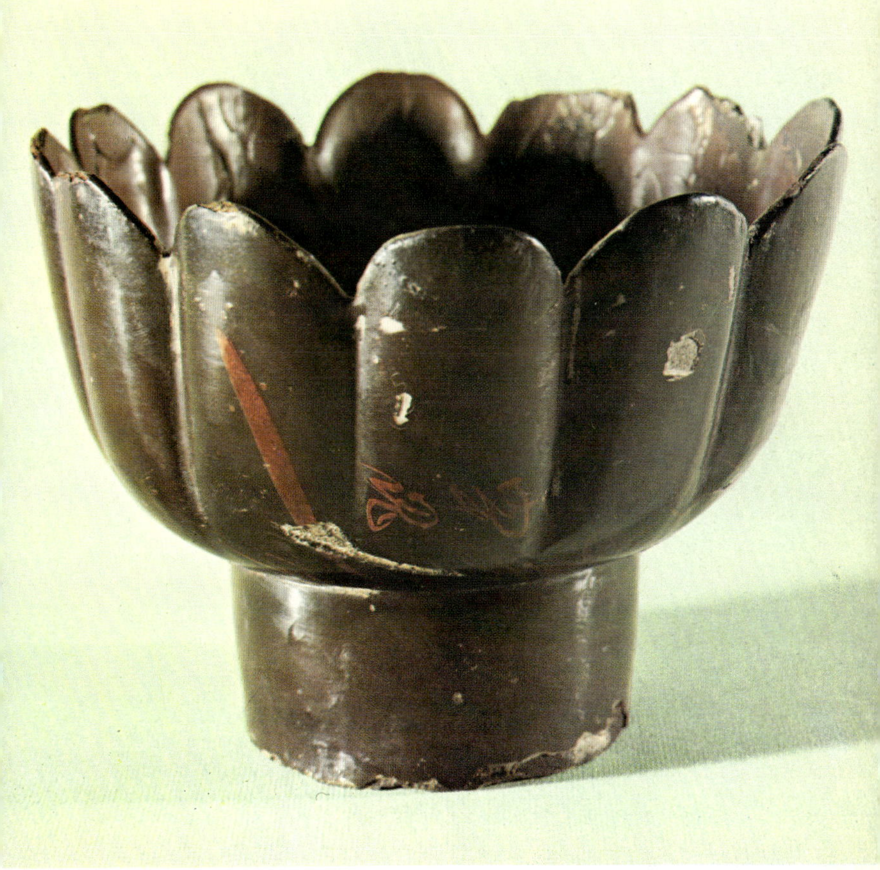

7. Bowl in the shape of a lotus flower. 10th-13th century. Musée Guimet, Paris.

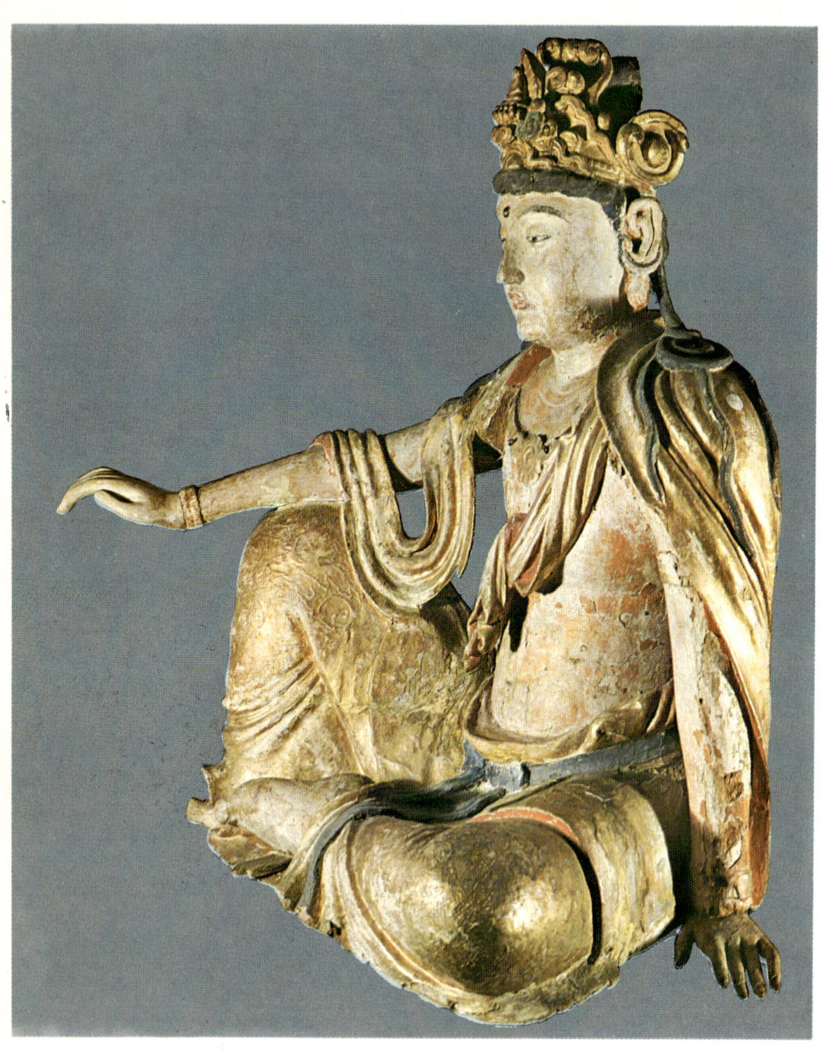

8. Large wooden statue. 12th-13th century. Private collection, Milan.

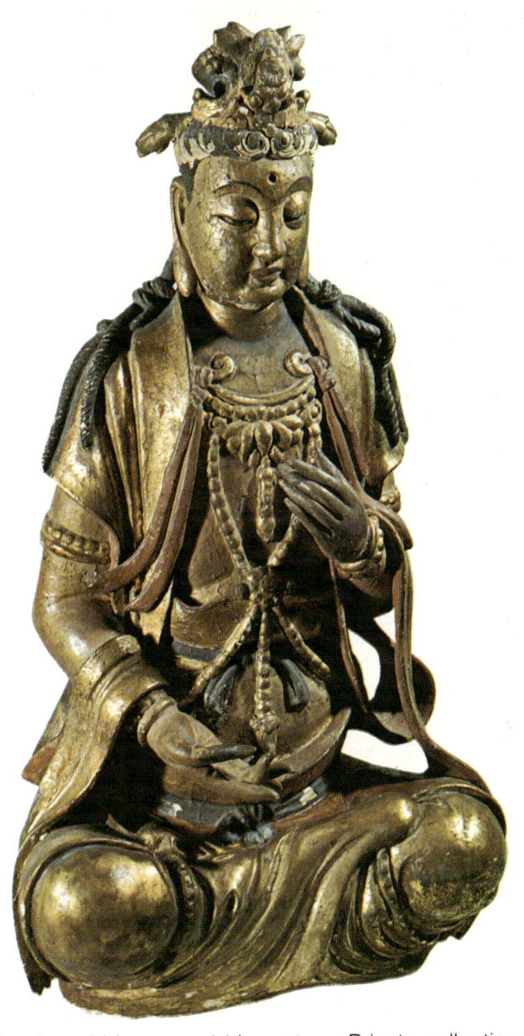

9. Statue in gold lacquer. 14th century. Private collection, Milan.

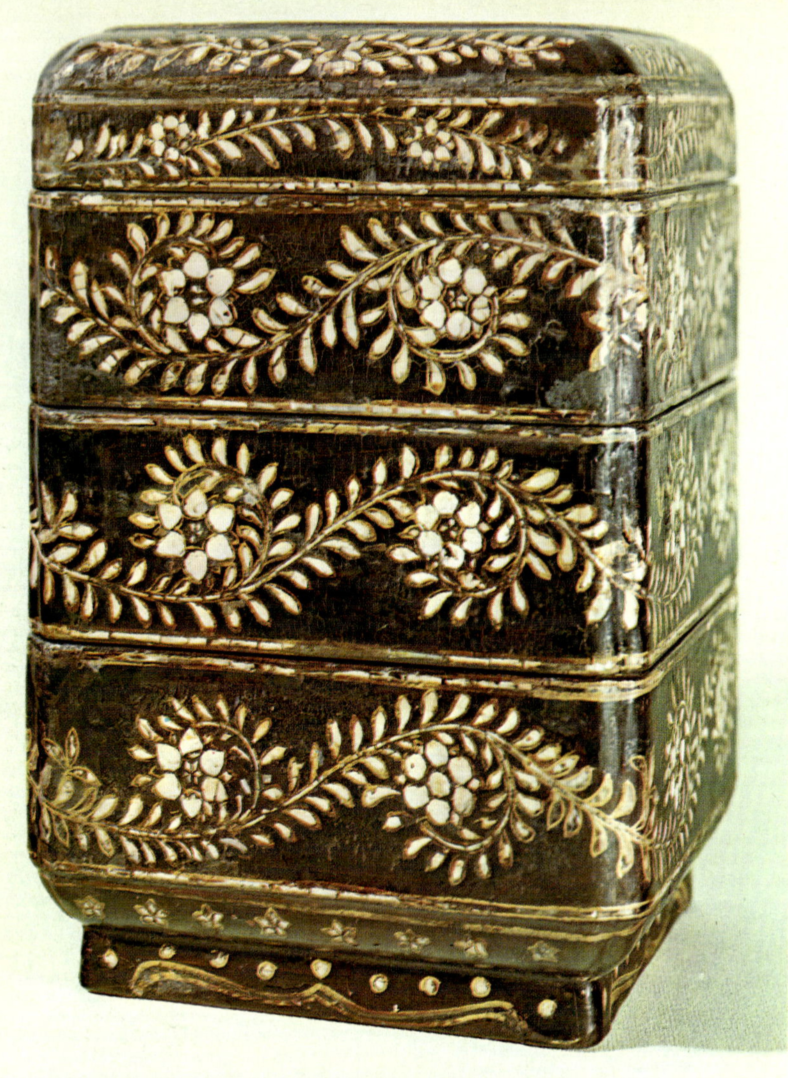

10. Box for sweetmeats. 18th-19th century. Musée Guimet, Paris.

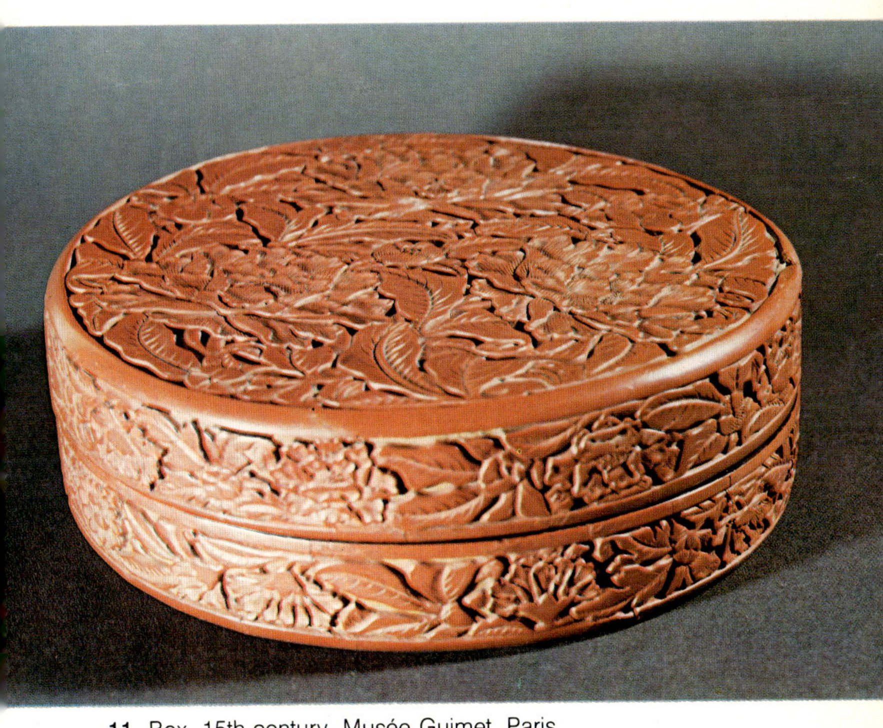

11. Box. 15th century. Musée Guimet, Paris.

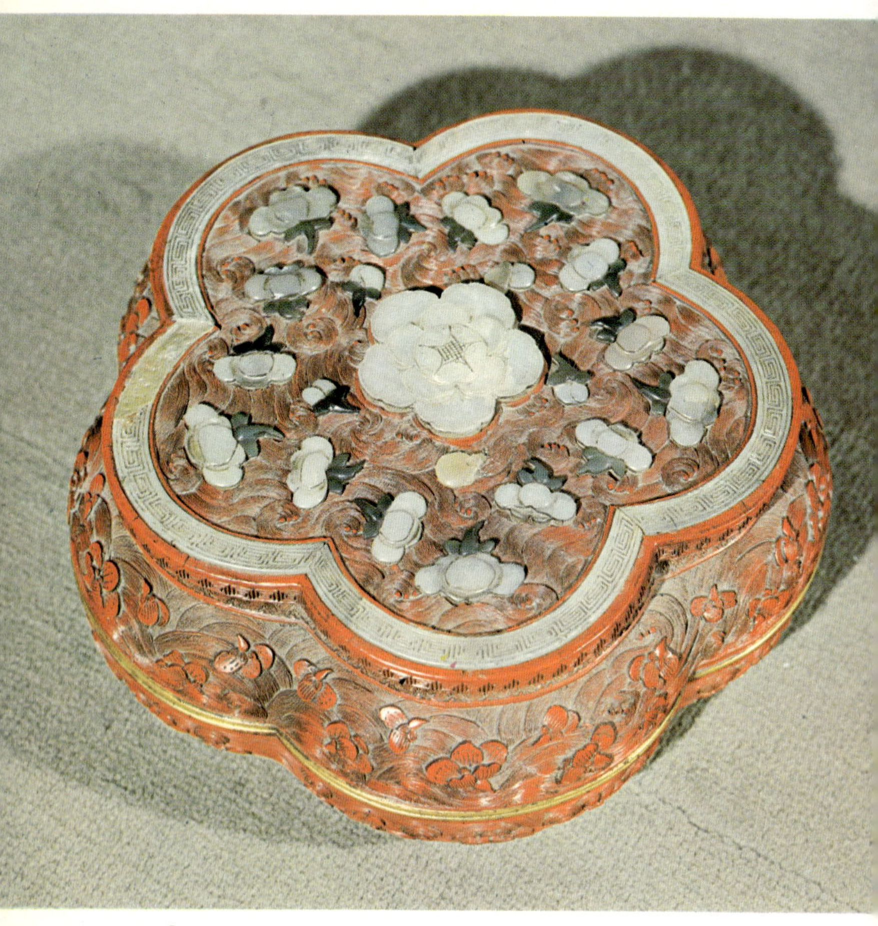

12. Cosmetic box. 18th century. Compagnie de la Chine et des Indes, Paris.

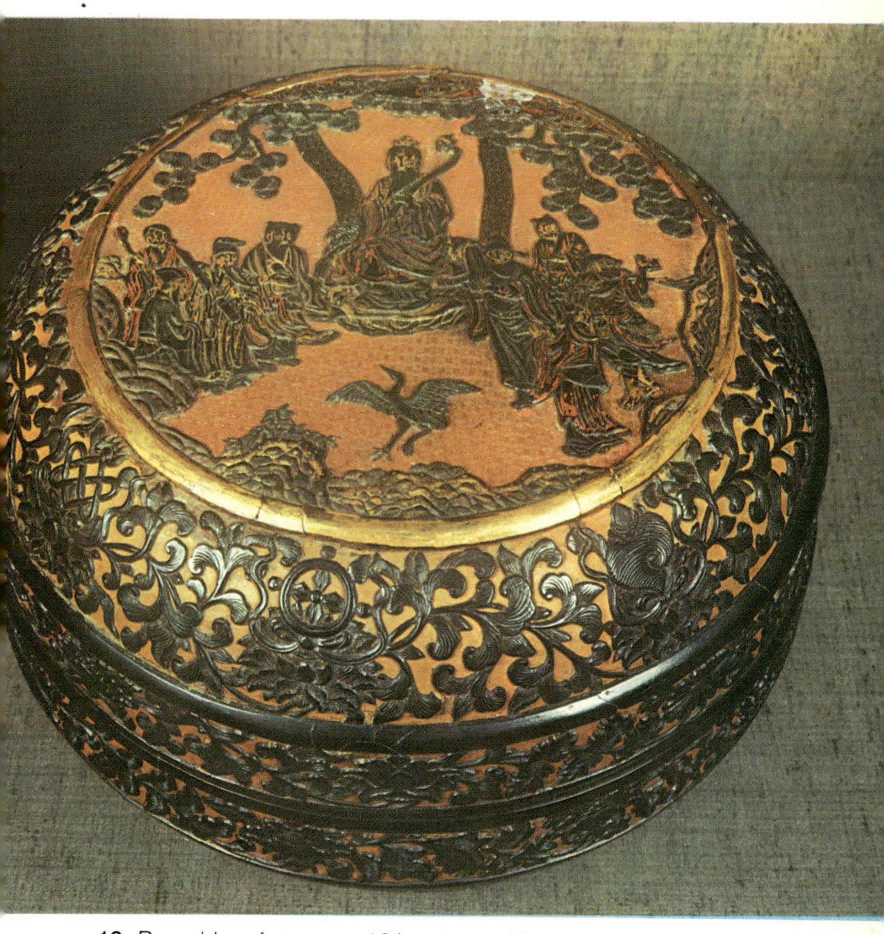

13. Round box for rouge. 16th century. Victoria and Albert Museum, London. Photo: John Webb.

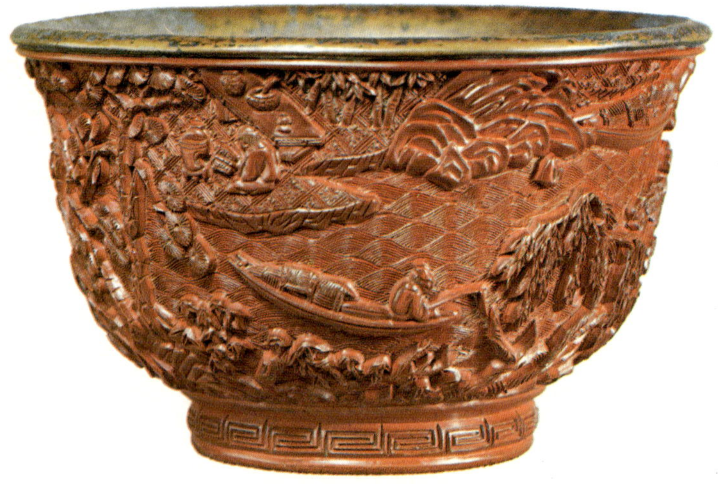

14. Lacquered metal bowl. 16th century. British Museum, London. Photo: John Webb.

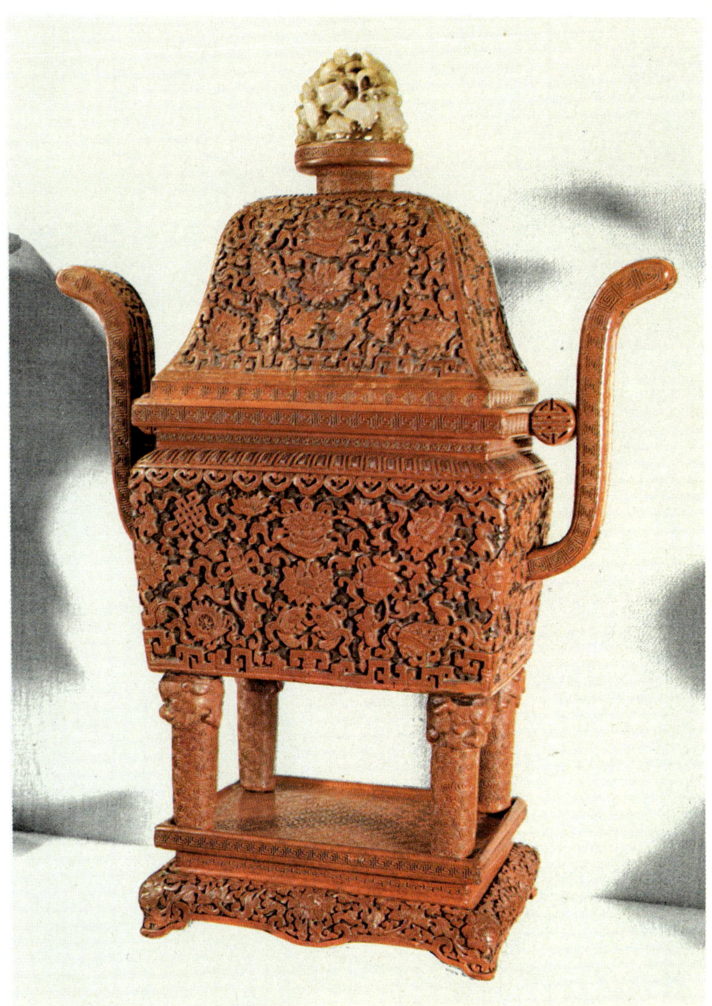

15. Vessel with lid. 16th-17th century. British Museum, London. Photo: John Webb.

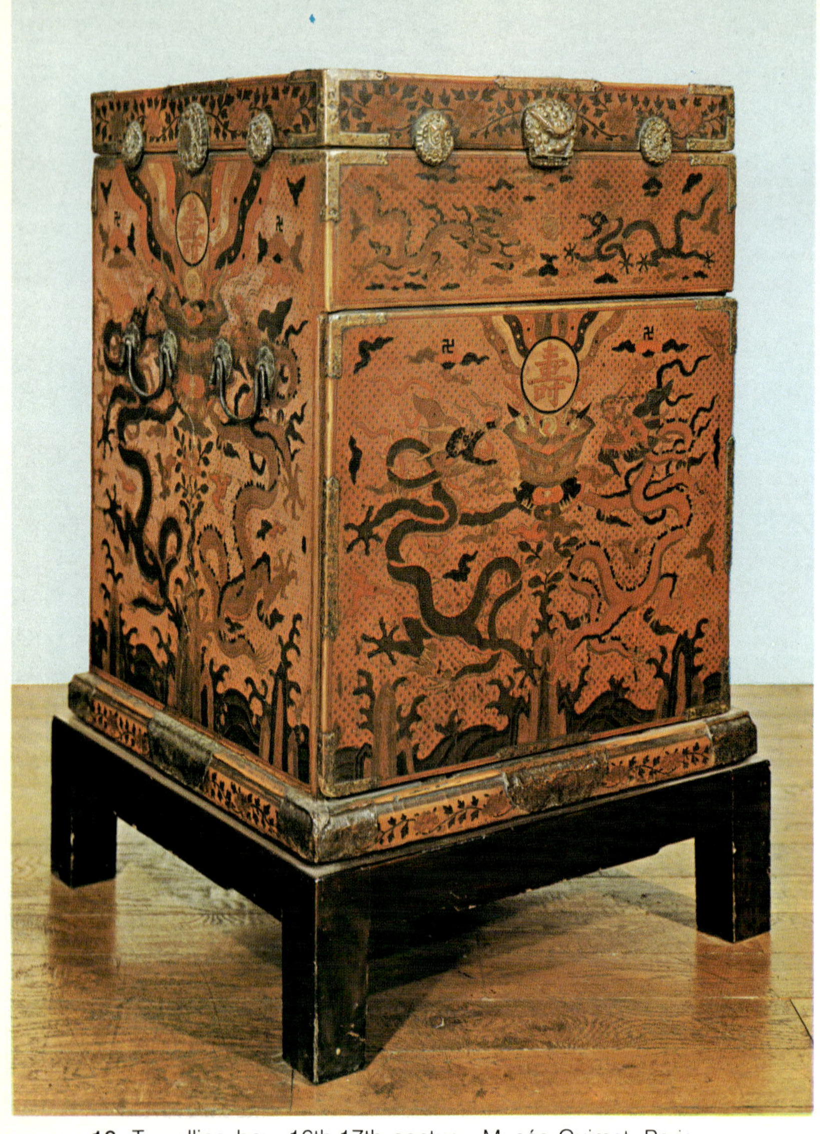

16. Travelling box. 16th-17th century. Musée Guimet, Paris.

political and military control over Lolang, the principal centre of production. Some of the workshops may have suffered in the struggles that took place during the establishment of the kingdom of Korea, and it is possible that many Chinese craftsmen made their way to Japan, where they received a warm welcome. The importance of the exodus of Chinese lacquer craftsmen to Japan is demonstrated by the number and variety of objects—purely Chinese in style—still preserved in the Shōsōin of the temple of Todaiji at Nara. The Shōsōin is a despository or store without windows rather than a museum, and holds the temple treasures. This treasure-house, still in an admirable state of preservation, was built by command of the Empress, widow of the Emperor Shōmu Tennō, at the time of his death in 756. Over 3000 objects of all kinds are kept there, including seventeen round drinking-cups in white lacquer painted in yellow and gold; various stringed instruments with lacquered figures and inlays of gold and silver as delicate as lace (the only intact specimens known); caskets, boxes and other objects, all splendidly lacquered and certainly of Chinese manufacture.

The T'ang and Sung periods (618-906 and 960-1279 respectively) are amply documented. There are descriptions of palaces decorated with polychrome and inlaid lacquer and containing lacquered furniture;

but no examples survive, and even less important objects are scanty and difficult to date. This is probably because, with the development of ceramics, pottery was used almost exclusively in tombs. Lacquered work was reserved for personal use, and therefore perished. Relatively fragile objects exposed to the air, and to the wear and tear of continual use, might easily fail to survive over a period of centuries; and political and military upheavals in China completed the work of destruction—the fall of the T'ang dynasty, the stormy period of the Five Small Dynasties (907-960), the far from peaceful Sung period, etc.

The Shōsōin of the Japanese temples, precisely because they were constructed without windows and were therefore immune from draughts and changes of temperature, were admirably suitable for preserving these collections, which were subjected to none of the wear of normal use. This explains an apparent paradox: that to establish the date of Chinese lacquers of the 7th-12th centuries, it is almost always necessary to compare them with specimens in Japan.

The only really satisfactory record of the art of lacquering on wood between the 11th and 18th centuries is provided by large statues, all of purely Buddhist inspiration. These were introduced by the Chin, the race of Khitan-Tartar origin who, between

1125 and 1280, defeated the Sung and occupied the greater part of the Chinese Empire to the north of the Yangtse-kiang. They rapidly adopted Chinese ways and became converted to Buddhism, and may be considered as the real initiators of wooden statuary in China. This art-form continued under the Mongol conquerors, the Yuan (1280-1368), and under the Ming (1368-1644), who restored national government to China. The statues usually represent a Kuan Yin. They have survived in good condition because they were jealously guarded in temples. As a result, it is relatively easy to distinguish the slight differences in treatment which characterise various periods. The Chin Kuan Yin, which are undoubtedly the most beautiful, have oval faces suffused with a withdrawn, seraphic peace; the bodies are relatively fine and slender, and they give a serpentine impression somewhat reminiscent of T'ang tomb figurines. It is from this period that my illustration (plate 8) comes. It is an example from my own collection, and is lacquered in gold and colours except for the hands and face; these are simply covered with a chalky dressing, partly worn away. The pose is the one favoured by the sculptors of the period, namely the attitude of 'regal repose'. The similar, even more beautiful statue in the Rijksmuseum in Amsterdam is of slightly later date. The one in the Metropolitan Museum of New York shows the first signs of the heaviness and 'baroque' quality of the Ming period; it is dated 1385, when the first Ming Emperor, Hung Wu, was on the throne.

Most modern authorities believe that the technique of inlaying with mother-of-pearl and ivory began in the T'ang period; but it seems to me that the perfect execution of certain T'ang works kept at Nara—particularly the lutes—suggests that the first attempts were much earlier. It is even more difficult to establish when Chinese craftsmen first produced incised lacquer work. All we know for certain is that the technique was widely used in the Yuan period; but in this case, too, its beginnings were probably much earlier. A well-known Chinese text, published in 1591, is *The Eight Discourses on the Art of Living* by Kao Lien, accurate transcriptions of which still exist. It says: 'During the Sung dynasty, incised lacquer was used to make small boxes for the Palace. The majority had a base [that is, the internal framework] of gold or silver covered with scores of layers of vermilion lacquer engraved with figures, palaces and plants; the skilled workmanship made them look as if they were painted. Lacquers of different colours were used and the carving was so deep that red peonies, green leaves and black rocks emerged in brilliant colour.' It ends by saying that these Sung works were already quite rare; so it is not surprising that they are unobtainable today. It is typical of the incongruities and contradictions so often encountered in the study of ancient Chinese texts that many of Kao Lien's statements about Sung lacquers are contradicted in another reliable work. Written in 1387 and republished in 1459, Ts'ao Chao's *Important Commentaries on Research into Antiquity* says: 'During the Sung dynasty, the objects for Palace use were of gold or silver covered with red lacquer and undecorated.' So far, none of these specimens of lacquer on a framework of precious metal has come to light, either with or without decoration.

Inlaid mother-of-pearl and ivory continued to be used, as did inlays obtained by using fine sheets of gold and silver cut into the shapes of flowers and leaves, and pierced lacquer shapes like the T'ang examples kept in the Shōsōin at Nara. The many Chinese texts describing Sung art are mainly devoted to painting and porcelain; but there are a few references to lacquering, despite the fact that it was regarded as no more than a craft. Anyone whose workmanship was particularly fine was mentioned. There is, for example, a note about the green lacquer which was made for the first time by a certain Chi Kung at the beginning of the 11th century in Chekiang, which is famous for its celadons. In his workshop, Chi Kung produced drinking-cups and wine beakers, small cosmetic boxes and other objects; all were very pleasing to the eye, although their beauty consisted solely in the perfection of their shape and the brilliance of the lacquer, since they were undecorated. This reference to the use of undecorated lacquer, like the quotation from Ts'ao Chao, is more readily understood if the characteristics of the Sung period are borne in mind. Throughout the period, China seems to have been shut in upon herself; Sung art displays a delicacy arising from the use of subtle colour and pure line which owes nothing to outside influence. There was probably a tendency in lacquer work also to abandon decorative styles, which during the T'ang period had been influenced by Middle Eastern styles, especially Sassanian silverware; and to imitate the wonderful monochrome simplicity of Sung pottery. In the Koechlin Collection in Paris, there are some lacquered boxes which are attributed to this period; they have black lacquer backgrounds and minute floral decorations in inlaid mother-of-pearl.

From the fall of the Sung dynasty (1279), Chinese art, including the art of lacquer, was marked by the greater heaviness and excess of decoration favoured by the Mongol Yuan conquerors. These 'barbarians' found themselves in contact with a civilisation infinitely superior to their own, and were eager to absorb it. They succeeded in doing so to a surprising extent, considering how short a time they ruled (little more than eighty years); but it seems that they found the delicate art of the Sung period too simple for their taste; like good *nouveaux-riches,* they preferred more display and gaudier decoration. The quality of lacquer probably deteriorated during this period; it had already found overseas markets and was made by speedier processes to keep up with the increasing demand.

In the *Eight Discourses,* Kao Lien writes: 'During the Yuan dynasty, new lacquer factories were opened. There was one in Chia Hsing where a large quantity of engraved red lacquer [*t' i hong* in the Chinese text] with reliefs was produced; but it lacked a hard brilliant surface and the background was almost always yellowish. These objects spoiled easily and the lacquer flaked off because the red layer was thin; so they are of little value. Things made for rich families were made more slowly, and the lacquer is therefore hard, brilliant and durable, like the ancient kind. Objects inlaid with mother-of-pearl [*li tien*] came from the workshops of Chi-an, which in ancient times used to work for the Emperor. Today these objects are not as hard-wearing. In the province of Yunnan [south-west China], from the Huan dynasty to this day, boxes have been made by carving in lime [this should probably be interpreted as 'modelling in white clay'] and covered with vermilion lacquer; but they are cheap and do not last long.'

Decorative statuettes, some of them very beautiful, were certainly made using dried mud covered with a layer of gold or polychrome lacquer. Because of their fragility, very few have survived, in spite of the external lacquering and the internal supports of fine metal wire. At an exhibition of Chinese art in Milan, I put on display a drinking-cup in a good state of preservation which represents two court ladies and is about 12 inches high. Better and more durable works were made by modelling in a mixture of ash, mud, fibres and vegetable oils which was exposed to the air, becoming extremely hard as it dried Once the statue was completely dry (but not fired), it was covered with lacquer. This method was most often used for larger sculptures, as in the example in plate 9 . It is a Kuan Yin some 27½ inches in height and, except for the hands, completely covered with a heavy gold lacquering which has remained intact. When I put it on show at the International Exhibition at Florence in 1963, I attributed it to the Yuan period; but a well-known English orientalist who saw it put forward the opinion that it was slightly later—perhaps from the first Ming period. I have therefore thought it best to avoid contesting the point by simply attributing it to the 14th century. In the absence of a known date, it is almost always impossible to determine whether a work belongs to the end of a given period or to the beginning of the next; there is nearly always a period of stylistic transition covering both.

In the Chinese chronicles alluding to the art of lacquering at the end of the Yuan period (14th century), reference is made to two artists, Ch'ang Chêng and Yang Mao. Both had workshops at Chekiang and produced works which were so delightful to look at that their fame reached Japan. Their speciality was deeply incised red lacquer. Little or nothing can be said about the Chinese lacquer produced during the reign of the first Ming Emperor, Hung Wu (1368-1398); apparently it was simply a continuation of the style and techniques of the previous period. Hung Wu was an austere personality with simple tastes; he was too busy restoring peace and prosperity to China (which had only just thrown off the foreign yoke) to take much interest in the arts.

The unfortunate Chien Wen (1398-1402), who was selected to succeed by his grandfather Hung Wu, reigned briefly before being killed by his savage uncle, Yung Lo. Yung Lo, Hung Wu's eldest son, reigned from 1402 to 1424. At the beginning of the reign, the Emperor of Japan took possession of all the lacquer objects acquired by Chinese and Japanese merchants from the workshops of Ch'ang Chêng and Yang Mao in Chekiang (the most easterly province of China and therefore the nearest to Japan). A Japanese ambassador was dispatched to the court of

Yung Lo with the customary gifts of recognition, and among the precious things he presented to the Chinese Emperor were some lacquered drinking-cups made by Ch'ang Chêng and Yang Mao. So it came about that, by a strange turn of events, works which had been made in China returned there as gifts from abroad. Yung Lo was agreeably surprised to find that works of such beauty were being made in his kingdom, and determined to invite the artist who had made them to come to the capital, which was now Peking. (The Chinese Emperor's ignorance is explicable by the low 'craft' status of lacquer work.) In the meantime, Ch'ang Chêng had died. His work was being carried on by his son, and it was therefore he who came to Peking (in about 1415) and became consultant at a lacquer works set up to provide for the needs of the court.

From the beginning of the 15th century, lacquer work was almost always red and incised; it later came to be known in Europe as Peking, or Imperial lacquer, although it was of course made in other provinces as well. The few pieces which can reliably be attributed to the Yung Lo period are some boxes and a splendid cylindrical vase belonging to the Chinese Nationalist Government, which exhibited it at the first exhibition of the treasures of the former Imperial Collection (London, 1935). On all of these pieces the incising is very clear-cut and deep; the lacquer itself is a deep vermilion. The decoration is almost always floral, but two round boxes, one in the Norton Collection in London and the other in the British Museum, carry figurative carvings in the lids which are identical in theme: a foreshortened view of a palace, with people leaning out of a veranda and others walking away into the distance; the whole framed in plants and clouds.

Ever since the 16th century, Chinese histories of art have described the great prestige enjoyed by red lacquers of the Yung Lo period, and how rare they became only a few decades after they had been made. At the beginning of the 15th century, lacquer workshops again received the attention of the Emperor, and at Peking at least one workshop was devoted to making things for the court. It thereby came under the supervision of an official overseer, which certainly ensured painstaking workmanship. Imperial supervision appears to have ceased at the death of the successor of Hsuan Tê (1425-1435).

The marks used during the reigns of Yung Lo and Hsuan Tê, the two golden ages of incised red lacquer, may sometimes be seen on small works shown in the larger Western collections; but it is hard to be sure that mark and object are of the same date, even though the object is authentic. An old Chinese book refers to a story about some lacquer workers in an Imperial workshop in the Hsuan Tê period. Their workmanship was pronounced below standard by the overseer, and in dismay at his criticism they cancelled the Yung Lo mark and substituted the Hsuan Tê mark. Authentic or not, the Yung Lo mark was always lightly scratched on, whereas the Hsuan Tê mark was incised or engraved and then filled with gold lacquer.

Other, though not always reliable texts mention an artist in the Imperial workshop in Peking who sent some of his assistants to Japan to study the evolution of lacquer work there, perhaps because he had heard of some new development. As a result, he started to produce magnificent works using lacquers of five colours which he mounted with filigree gold, using a special new technique. Some of these, all of exquisite workmanship, are on show in Western collections. They probably belong to the Hsuan Tê period, although this can be challenged since, so far as I know, none of them possesses a date-mark.

Some commentators have claimed that the red of Yung Lo lacquer was deeper and more brilliant than that of the Hsuan Tê period. Such assertions cannot be unreservedly accepted; for though the slight differences may have been there from the beginning, it cannot be a matter of certainty. However fast the colours of ancient lacquers, more or less exposure to light may have caused slight alterations over the centuries.

There was a notable increase in the output of

lacquer throughout the 16th century, and private-enterprise workshops sprang up in many provinces. It is, however, generally believed that the best were still those of Peking, despite the cessation of official control. Decoration became more varied, though the technique of engraving took pride of place over inlay and painting techniques. The subjects, which had at first been almost exclusively floral, came to include figures, landscapes and animals. In very general terms, it may be said that the design tended to become more crowded, and that a more vigorous and personal art was sacrificed to the search for greater complexity and perfection of technique.

As the use of lacquer spread, it ceased to be the prerogative of the rich and powerful. Factories sprang up to cater for the everyday needs of the less wealthy. In such factories the lacquering was not done by the costly and long-drawn-out process described in the first chapter. The lacquer was probably given a deep colour by the use of drying oils and other inexpensive substances, laid on with a spatula, incised in somewhat rough and ready fashion, and smoothed over only once, at the end of the operation. In both these 'provincial' lacquers and the more sophisticated ones, different coloured lacquers were sometimes inserted into the spaces left empty by the carving. Once the piece was dry, it was smoothed down so that this inlay of lacquer upon lacquer looked as if it had been painted.

Towards the end of the Ming period, the fashion of painting in lacquer on a predominantly black background became very popular, and the painting was sometimes carried out by great artists. Inlaid mother-of-pearl was frequently used to set off the painting. During the Chia Ching (1522-1566) and Wan Li (1573-1619) periods, there was a considerable output of lacquer work. Almost all the furniture owned by rich families was lacquered, and a typical lacquering technique at the end of the 16th century was to cover wood with a coarse cloth with a lacquering the colour of old leather, thickly decorated and lightly incised; the technique was used for tables and wardrobes in particular.

Chia Ching was deeply interested in red incised lacquer work. It is certain that during his reign at least one Imperial factory was re-established in Peking to supply the court with this type of work. Some authors maintain that the not uncommon decoration which represents a five-clawed dragon proves that the work on which it appears was intended for Imperial use. This is likely, but not irrefutable. There were various edicts which reserved certain materials and symbols for the court and prohibited their use for the common people. Among them is one which declares that the five-clawed dragon (an emblem of sovereignty) was not to be embroidered or otherwise depicted on fabrics not intended for the exclusive use of the Emperor; but there is no mention of its prohibition as a decoration on other materials.

The incising techniques used during the Chia Ching period achieved clarity and depth, making equal use of sharp and rounded edges. It was in this period, too, that a method which had fallen into disuse came back into fashion. This was the technique of lacquering in alternate layers of different colours, all of which were made visible by the carving. These lacquers are known in Europe by the name *guri*, a term coined by the Japanese to describe a similar product of their own. With the enormous increase in output during the long reign of Wan Li (1573-1619), the art of lacquering entered a phase of marked decadence. Decorations tended to become confused and formalistic, and the lacquers incised with clear, sharp edges that gave them an almost sculptured appearance disappeared. Little is known about Chinese art during the politically chaotic period between the end of Wan Li's reign and the first year of the reign of the great Emperor K'ang Hsi (1662-1722). In the absence of dated works it is therefore difficult to distinguish between lacquers of that period and those of the succeeding Yung Chêng period (1722-1735).

An important innovation in 17th-century China

was the manufacture of the great screens famous in Europe under the name of a city in India: Coromandel screens. Why they should be so called is a mystery; many people believe the name derives from the port from which the screens were dispatched to the West, but even this is uncertain. In outline, the method by which they were made was as follows. The workmen took thin sheets of pinewood and placed a fine cloth on them. A mixture of vegetable glue and slate which had been finely powdered in a mortar was then laid on with a spatula to make the cloth stick to the wood. When the whole thing was dry, the surface was levelled by rubbing it down with a small hempen bag filled with ash. When a mirror-like surface had been created, the lacquering could begin; several layers were applied, until the lacquer was about an eighth of an inch thick. Then the artist cut his design on the lacquer, gradually engraving it deeper and deeper but taking care not to cut into the wood. Tempera colours were then put into the incisions, drop by drop. The pieces of wood were mounted on a frame which was in turn decorated with painted lacquer or inlaid with mother-of-pearl, and joined to other sections with rudimentary clasps. This colouring of the engraving was generally carried out on only one side of the panel; the other was simply lacquered with a decoration of gilded linear designs. Sometimes the panels

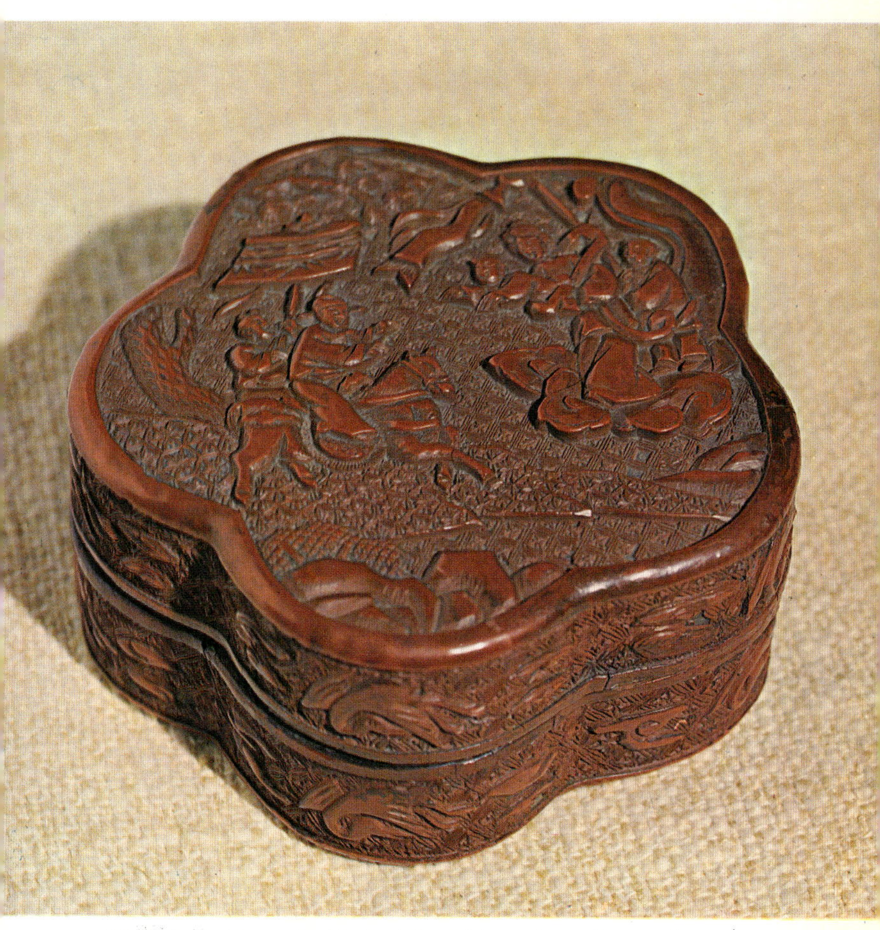

17. Lobated box. 2nd half of the 16th century. Fernanda Sona Collection, Milan.

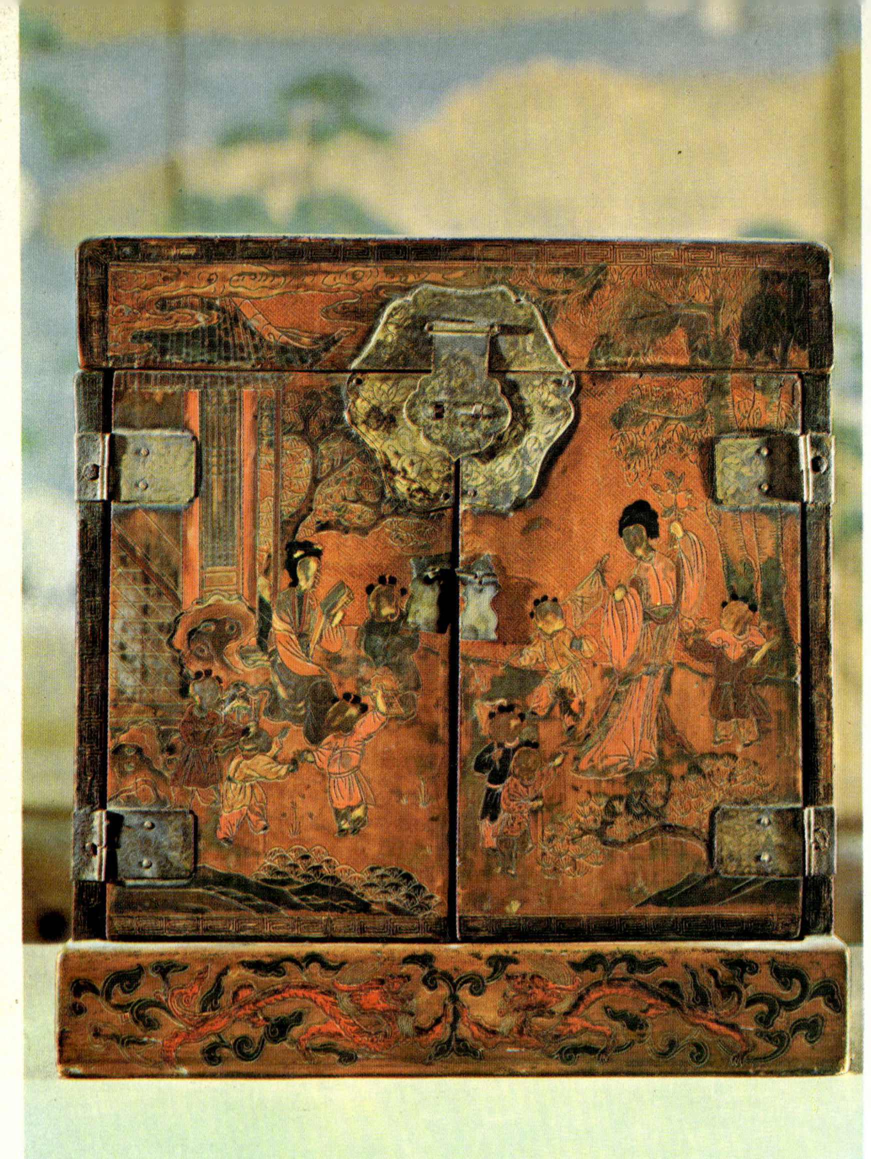

18. Cabinet with two doors. 16th century. Compagnie de la Chine et des Indes, Paris.

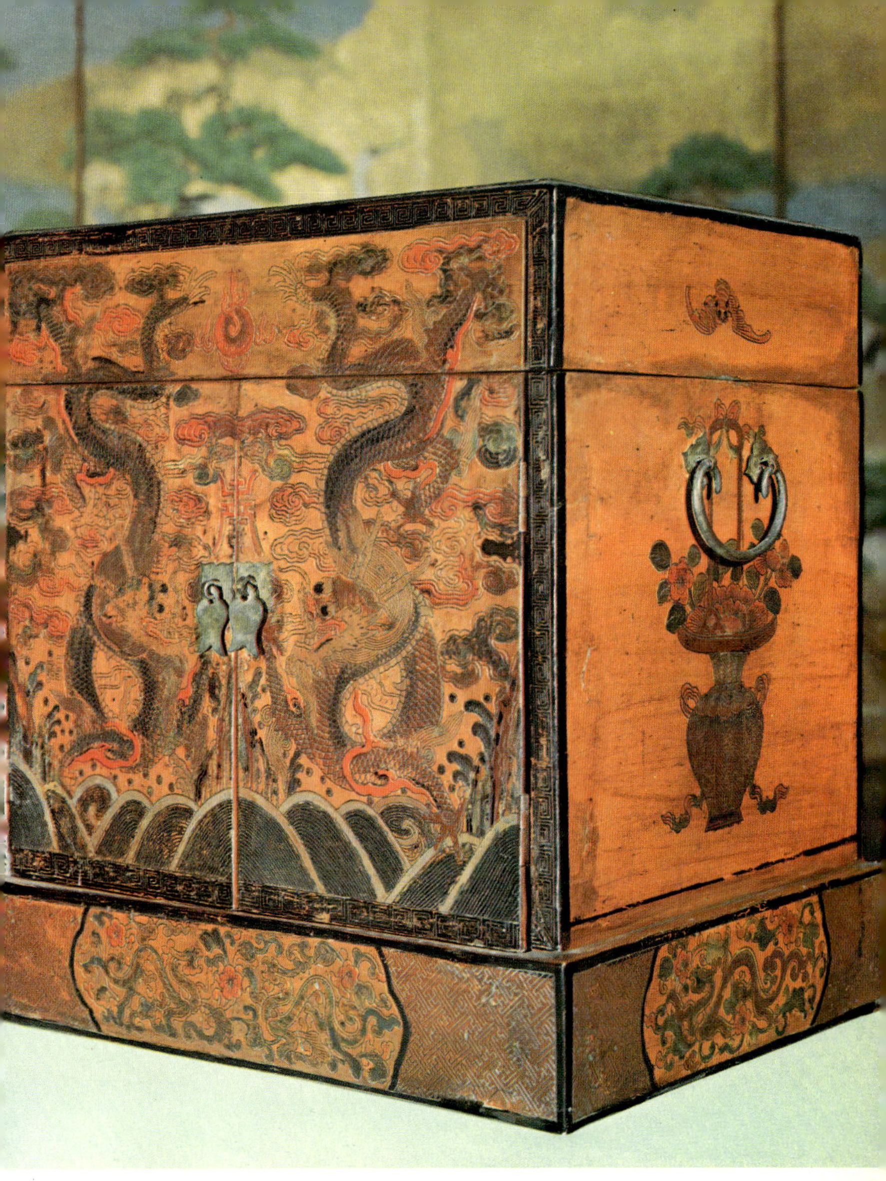

19. Red lacquered coffer. 17th century. Compagnie de la Chine et des Indes, Paris.

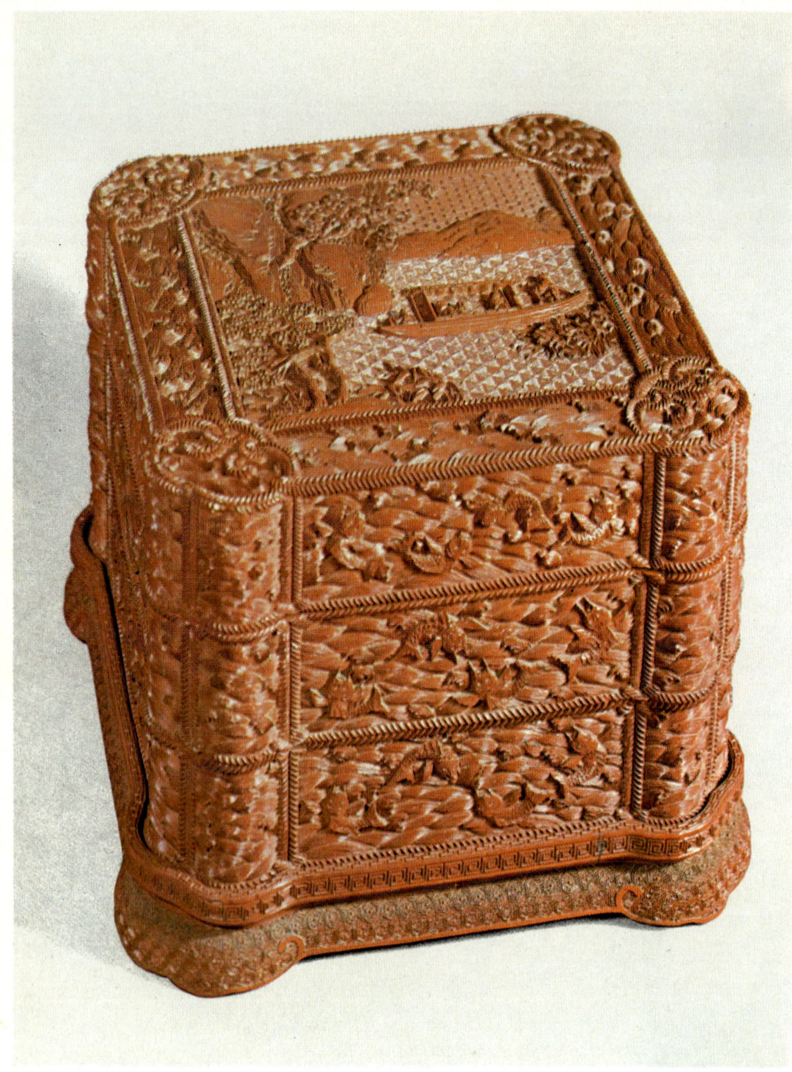

20. Lacquered wood casket. 16th-17th century. British Museum, London. Photo: John Webb.

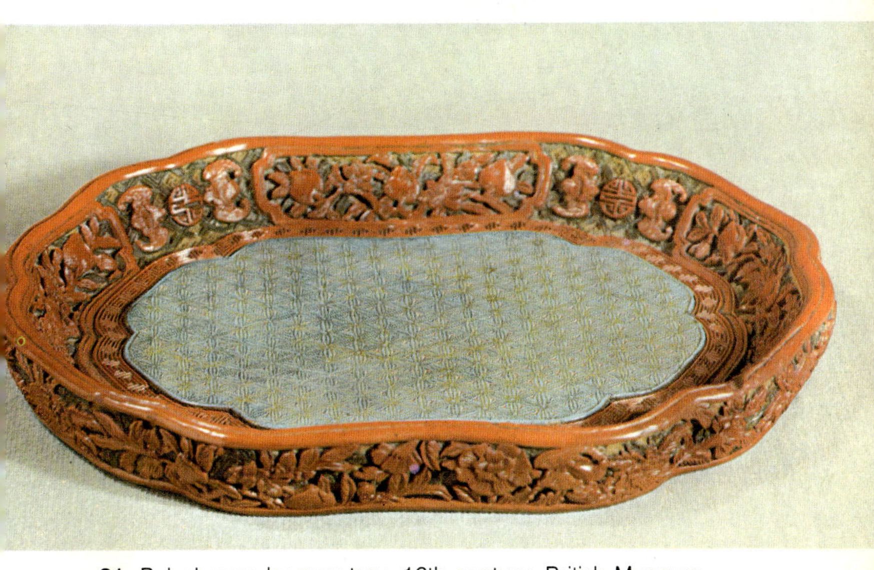

21. Polychrome lacquer tray. 16th century. British Museum, London. Photo: John Webb.

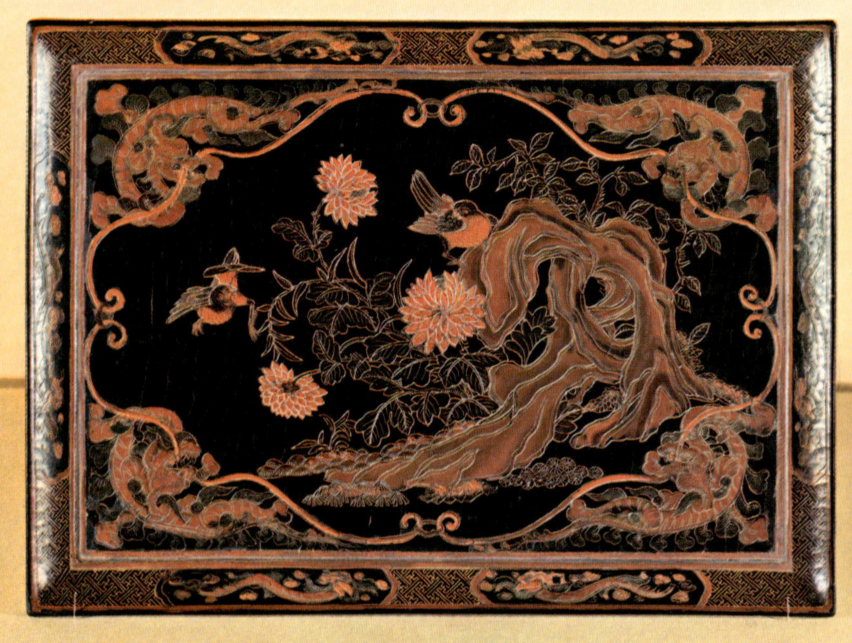

22. Tray. 16th-17th century. Cornelia Blakemore Warner Fund, Cleveland Museum of Art, Cleveland.

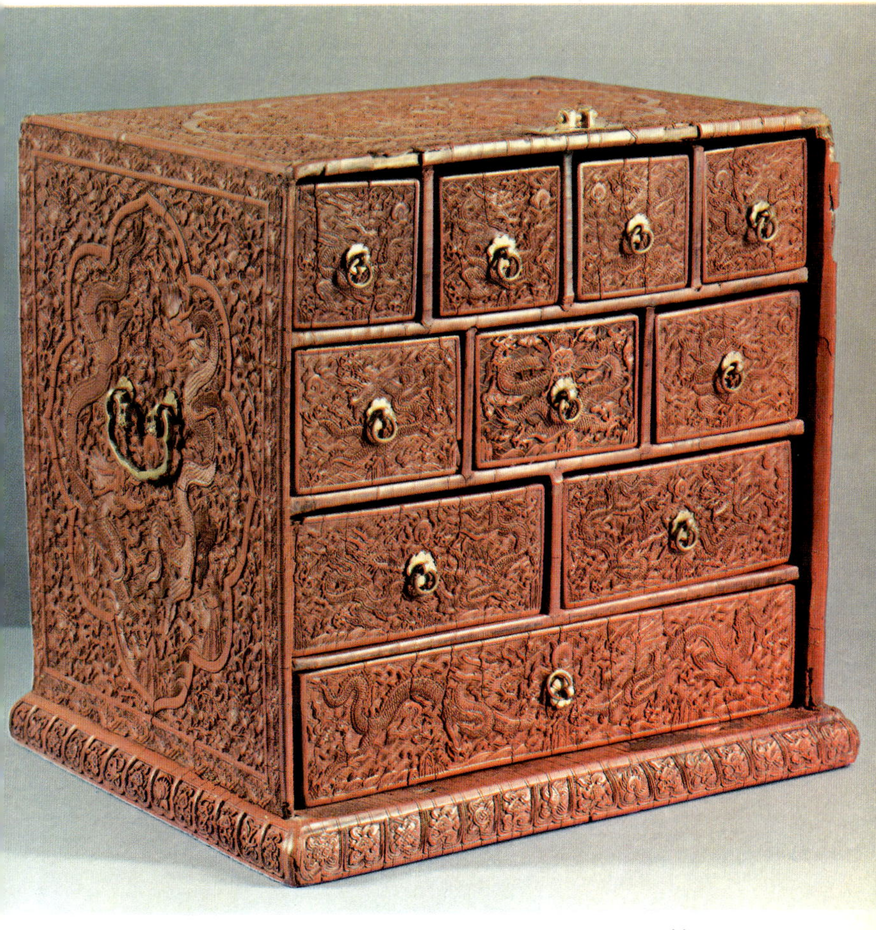

23. Cabinet with several compartments. 16th century. Norman O. Stone and Ella A. Stone Memorial Fund, Cleveland Museum of Art, Cleveland.

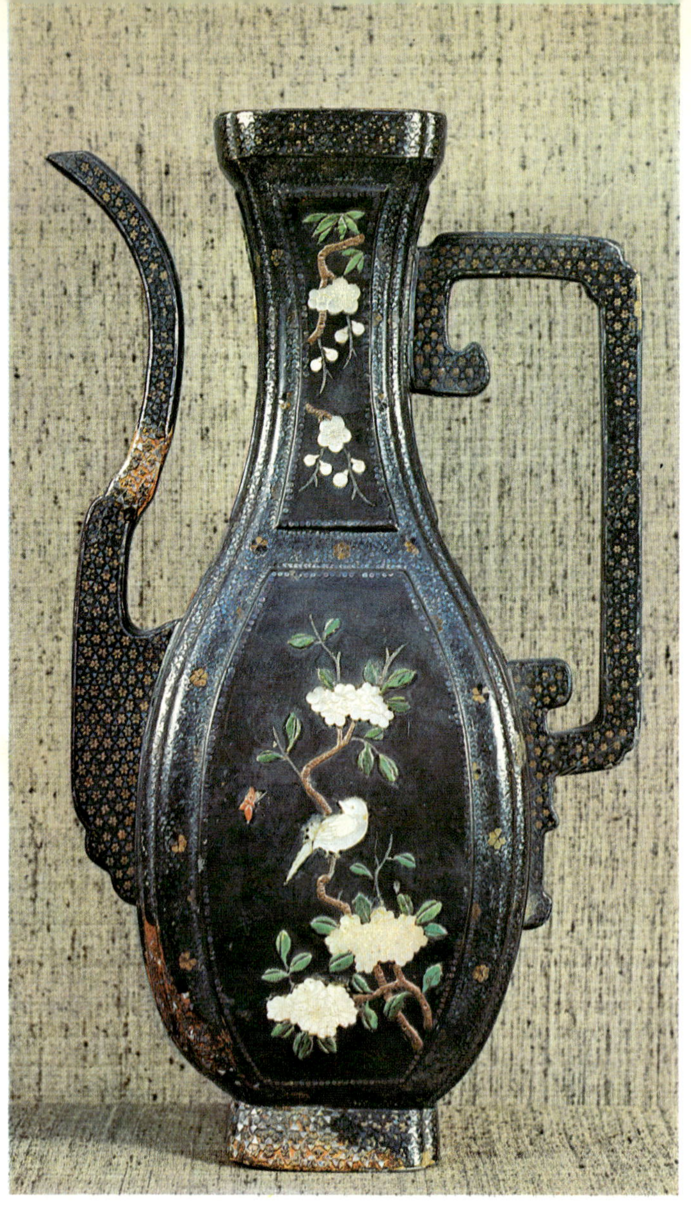

24. Wine jug. 16th-17th century. Victoria and Albert Museum, London. Photo: John Webb.

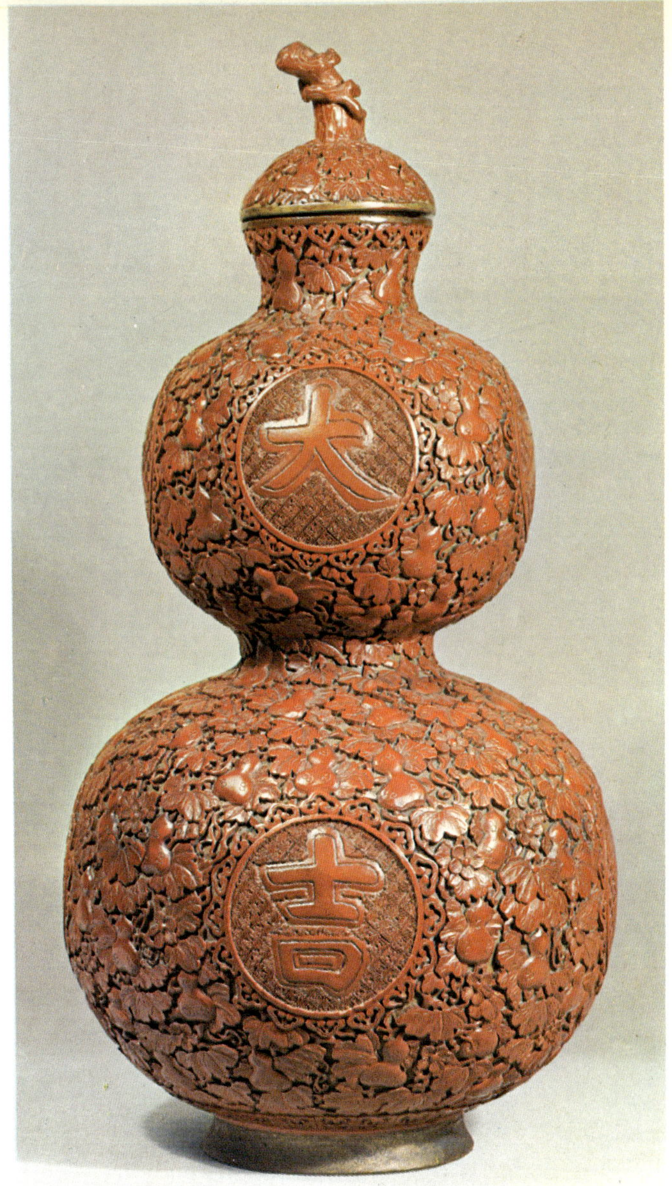

25. Double container. 16th-17th century. British Museum, London. Photo: John Webb.

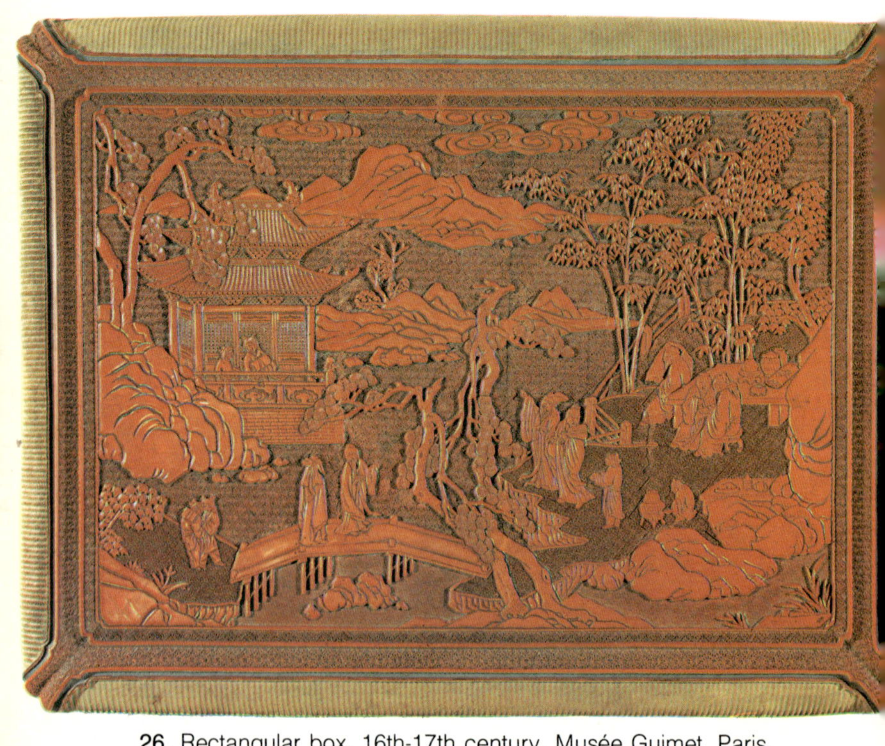

26. Rectangular box. 16th-17th century. Musée Guimet, Paris.

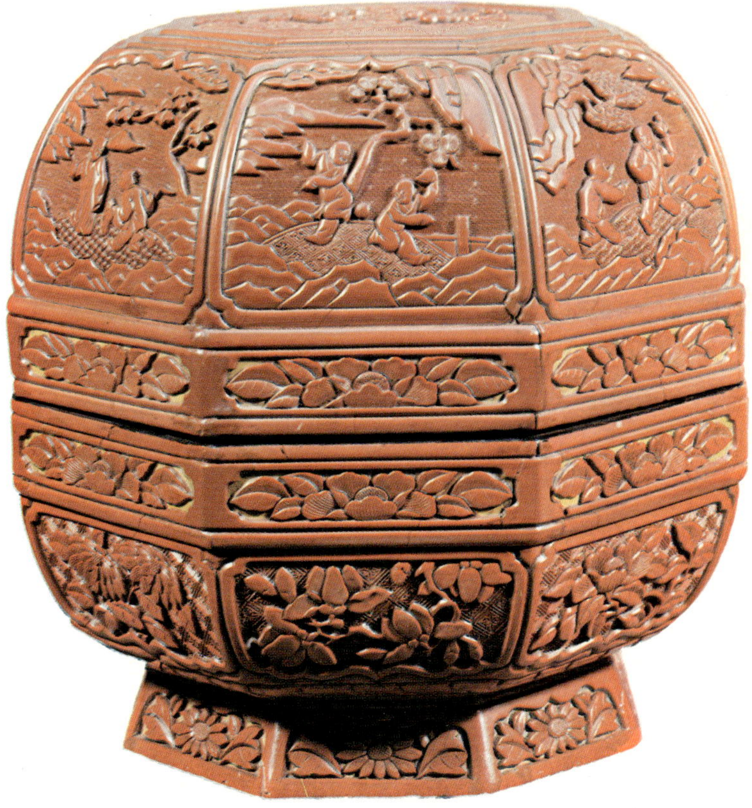

27. Hexagonal casket with lid. 17th century. Victoria and Albert Museum, London. Photo: John Webb.

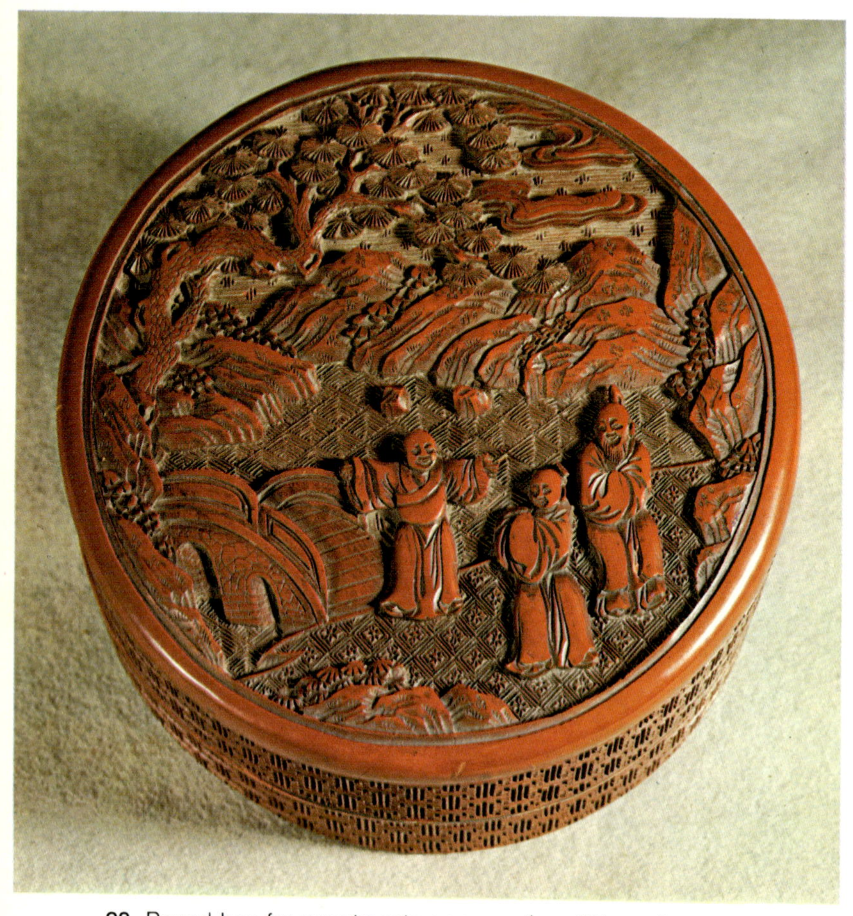

28. Round box for sweetmeats or cosmetics. 17th century. Zlata Kovacevic Collection, Milan.

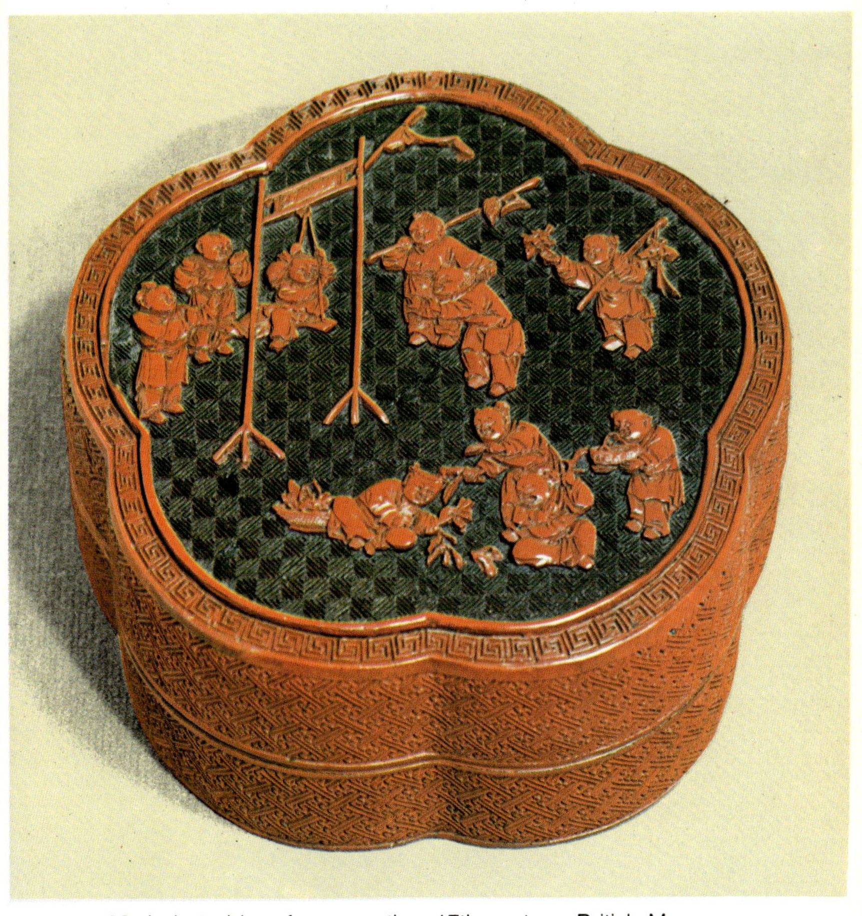

29. Lobated box for cosmetics. 17th century. British Museum, London. Photo: John Webb.

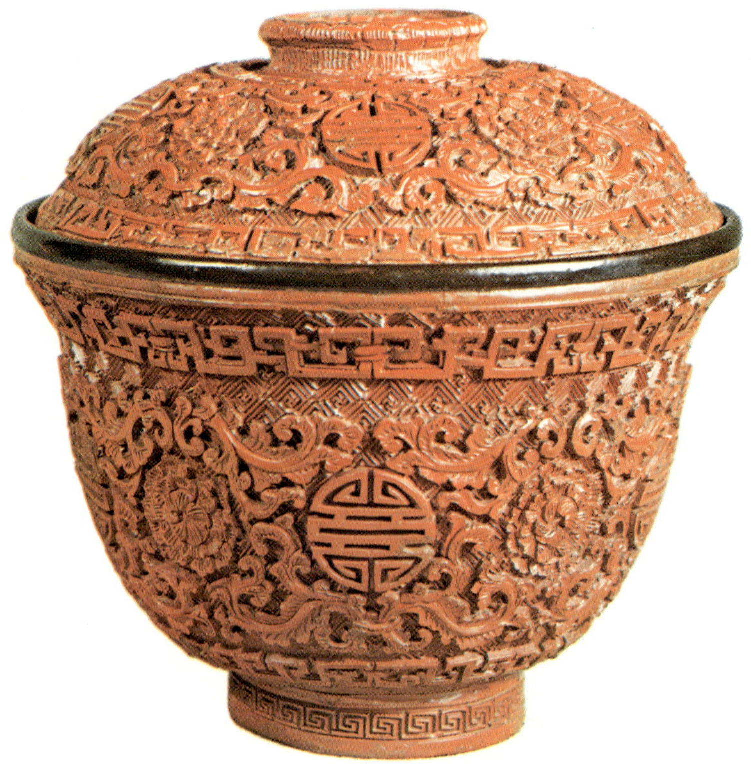

30. Round bowl with lid. 17th century. British Museum, London. Photo: John Webb.

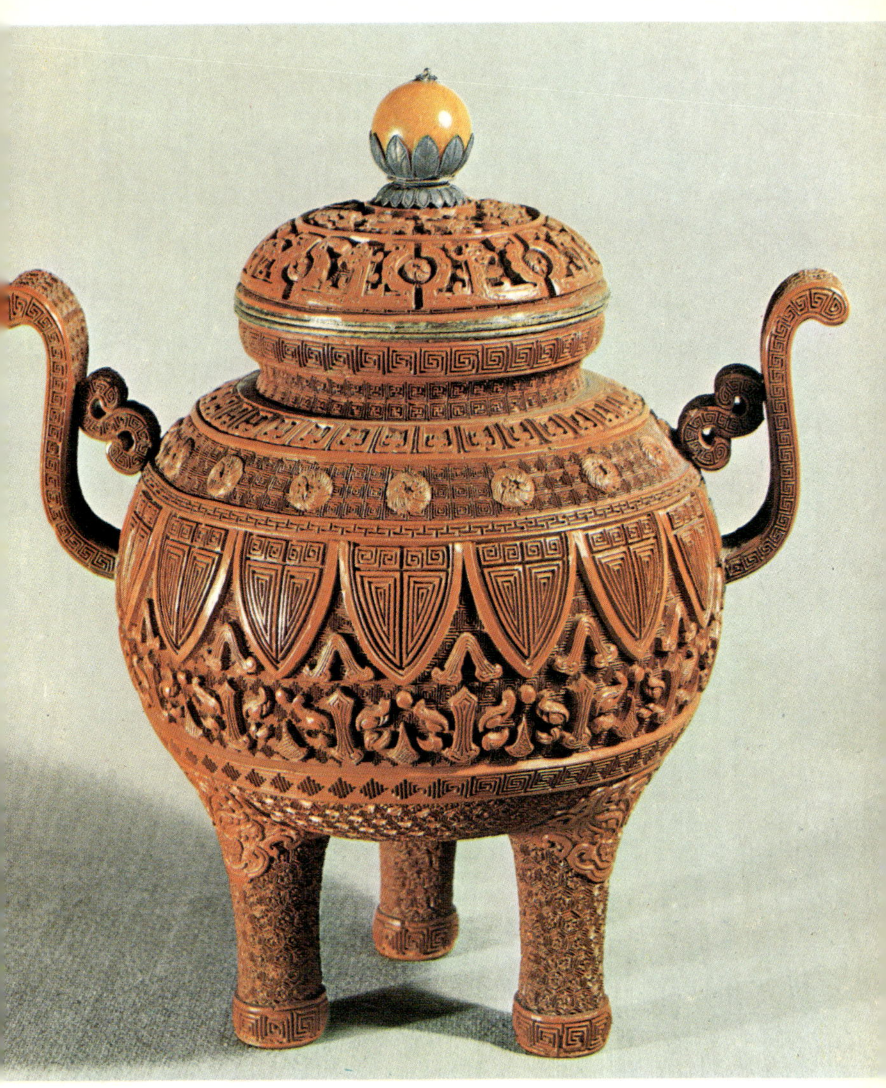

31. Censer. 17th century. British Museum, London. Photo: John Webb.

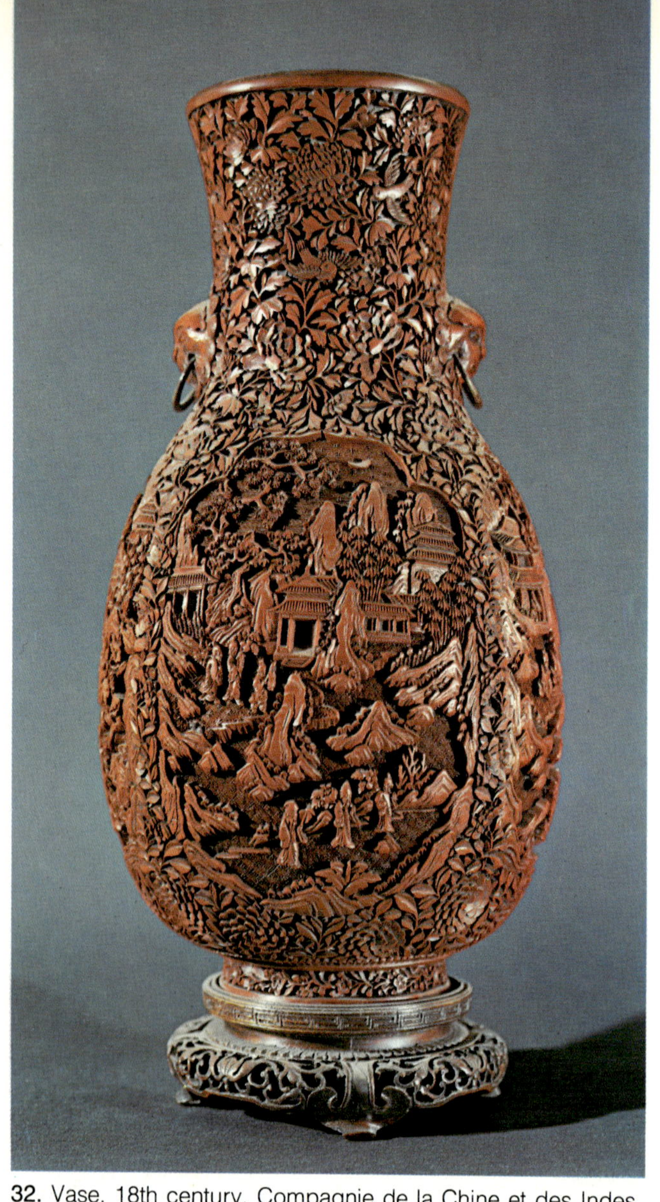

32. Vase. 18th century. Compagnie de la Chine et des Indes, Paris.

33. Rectangular tray. 17th century. Victoria and Albert Museum, London. Photo: John Webb.

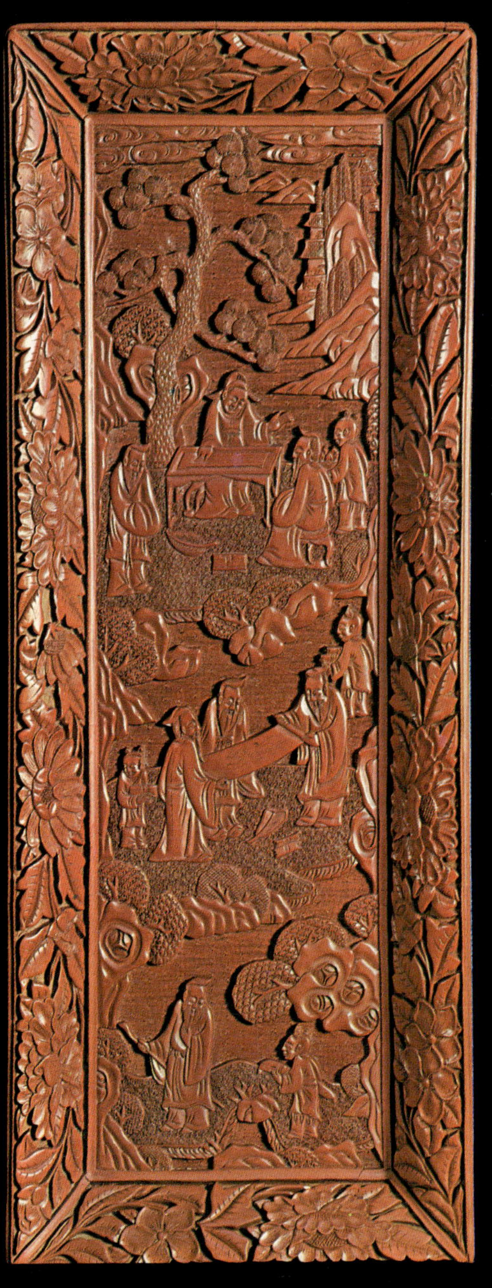

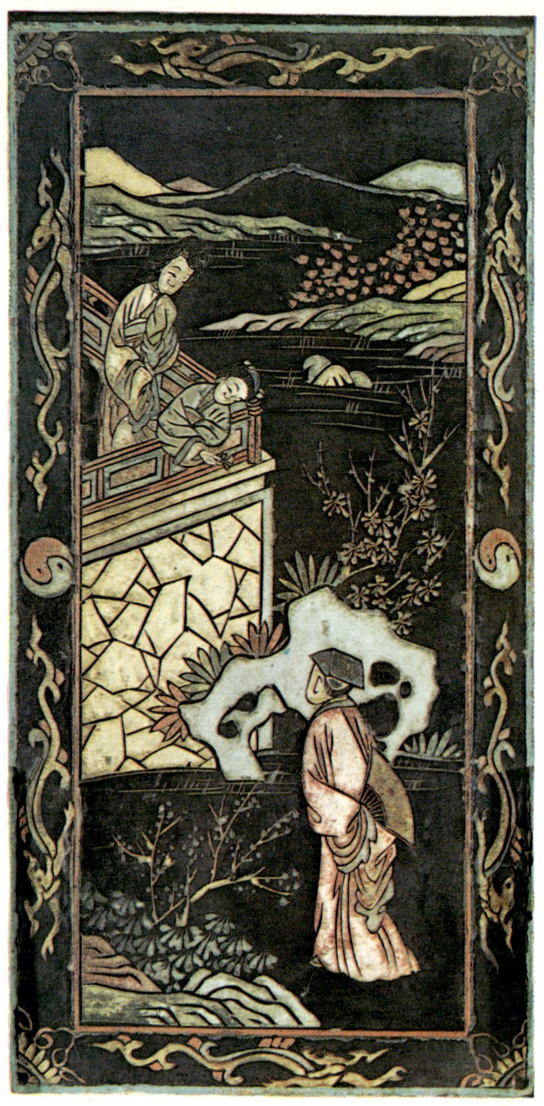

34. Screen in Coromandel lacquer. 17th-18th century. Compagnie de la Chine et des Indes, Paris.

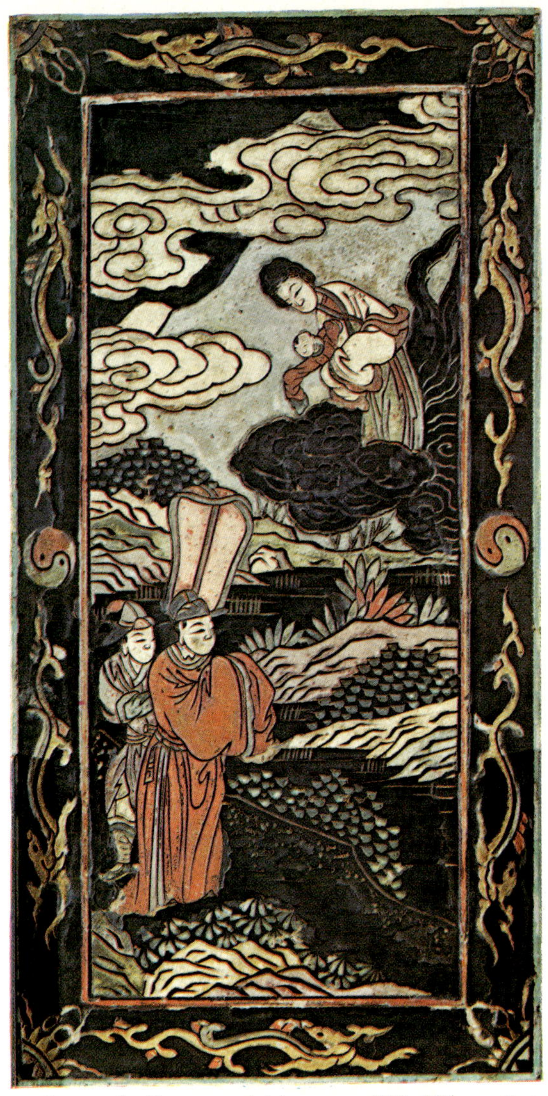

35. Screen in Coromandel lacquer. 17th-18th century. Compagnie de la Chine et des Indes, Paris.

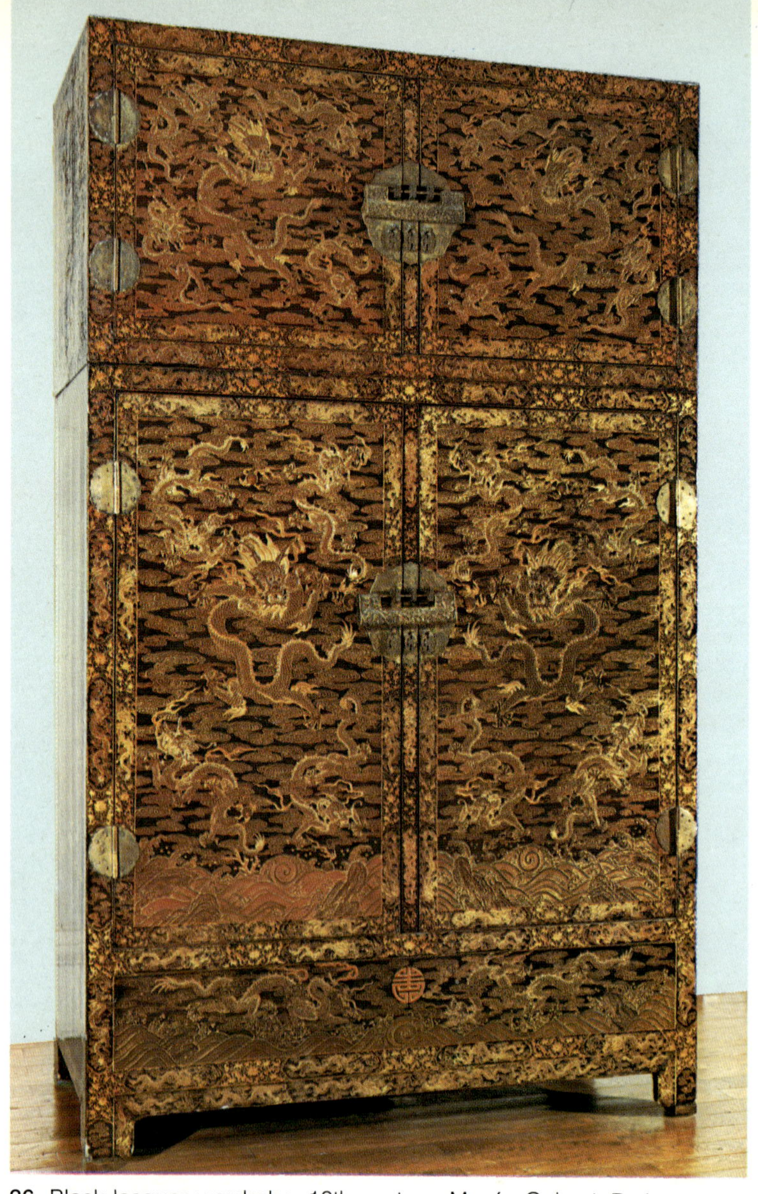

36. Black lacquer wardrobe. 18th century. Musée Guimet, Paris.

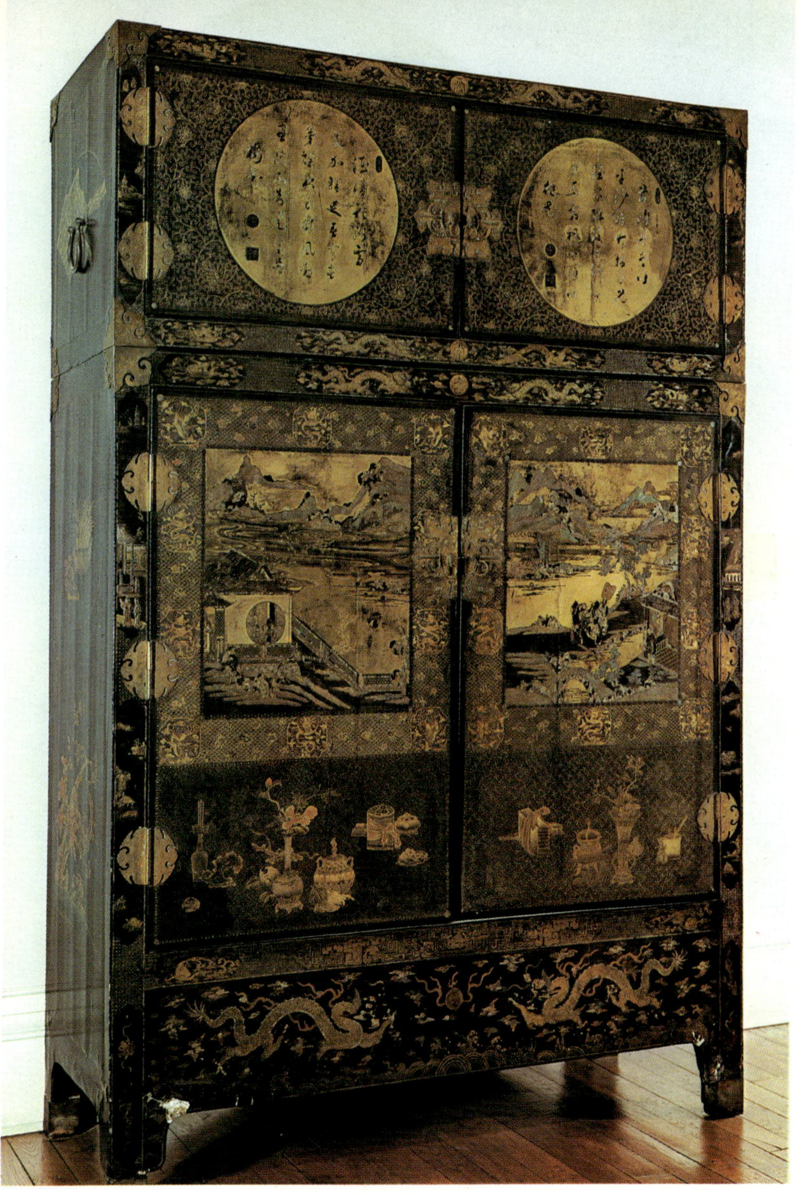

37. Black lacquer wardrobe. 17th-18th century. Musée Guimet, Paris.

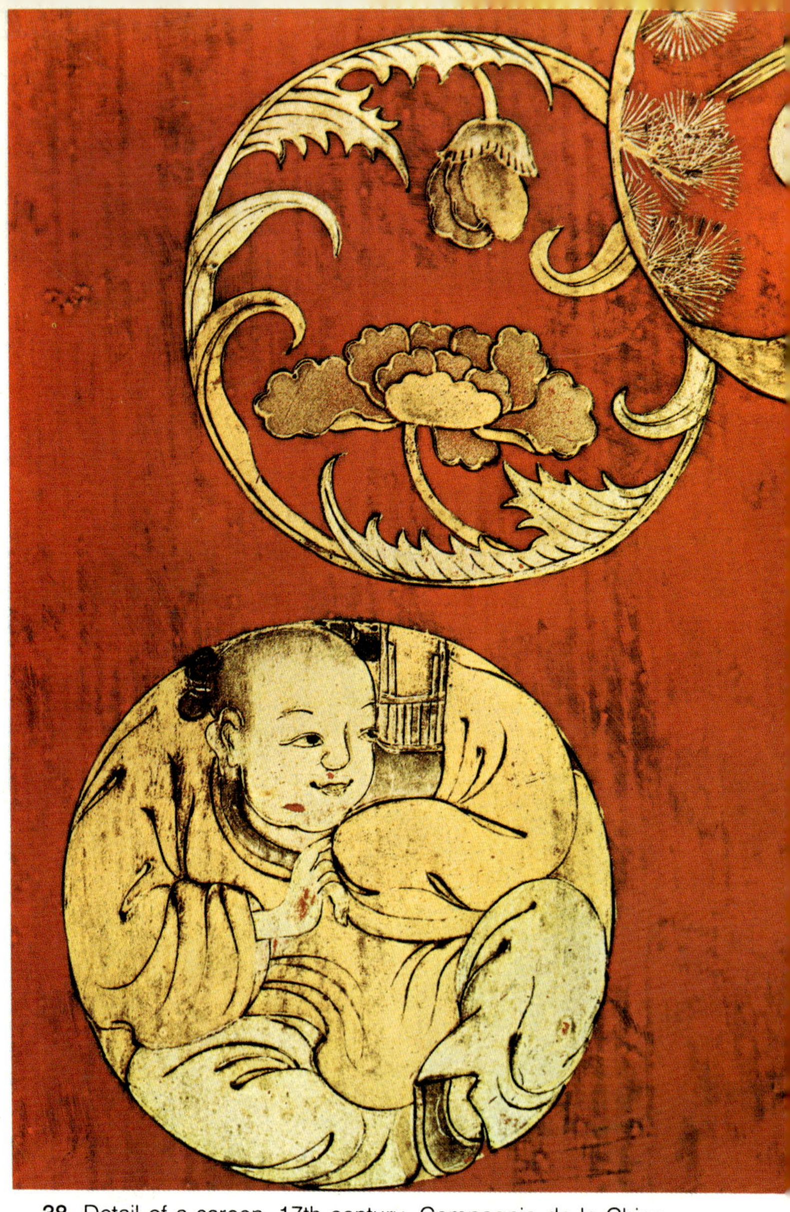

38. Detail of a screen. 17th century. Compagnie de la Chine et des Indes, Paris.

39. Lacquered wardrobe. 18th century. Victoria and Albert Museum, London. Photo: John Webb.

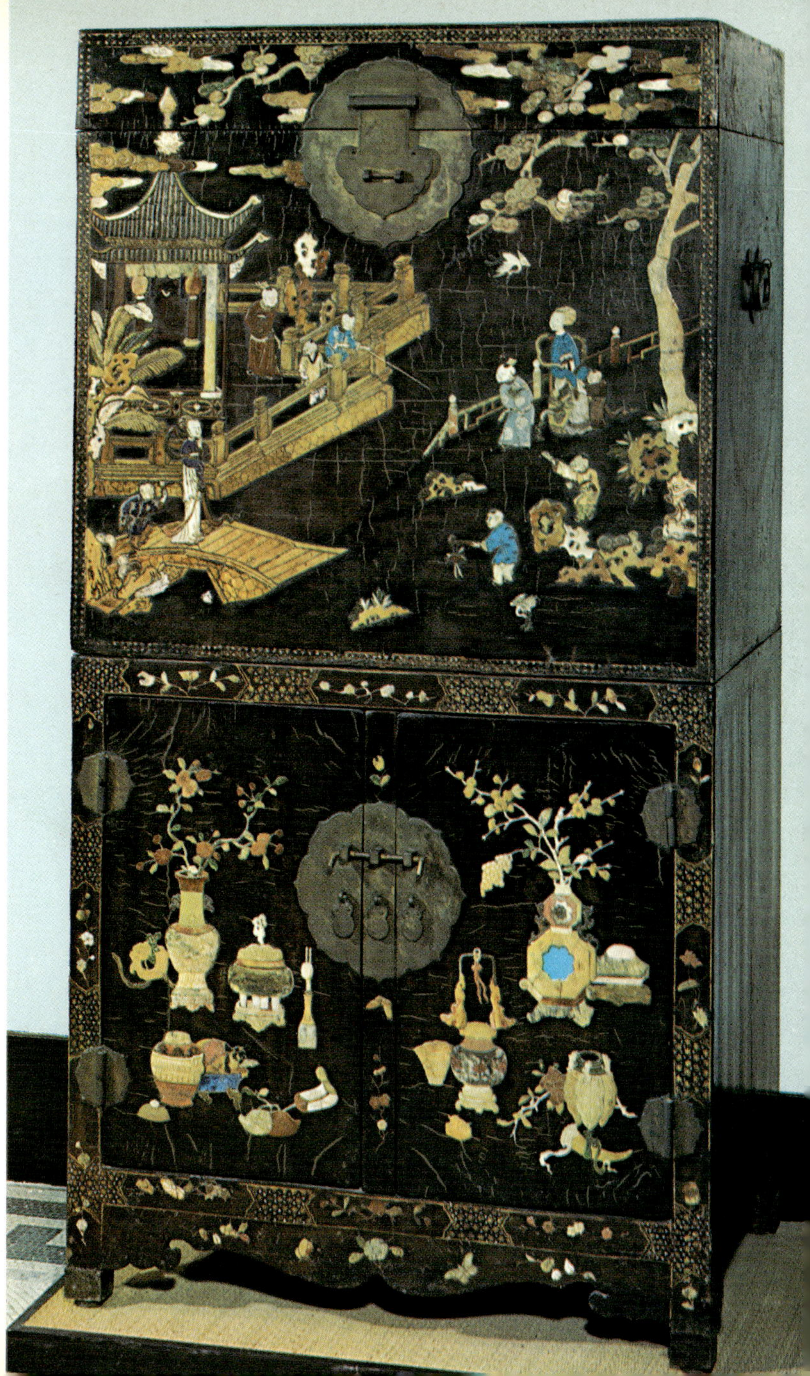

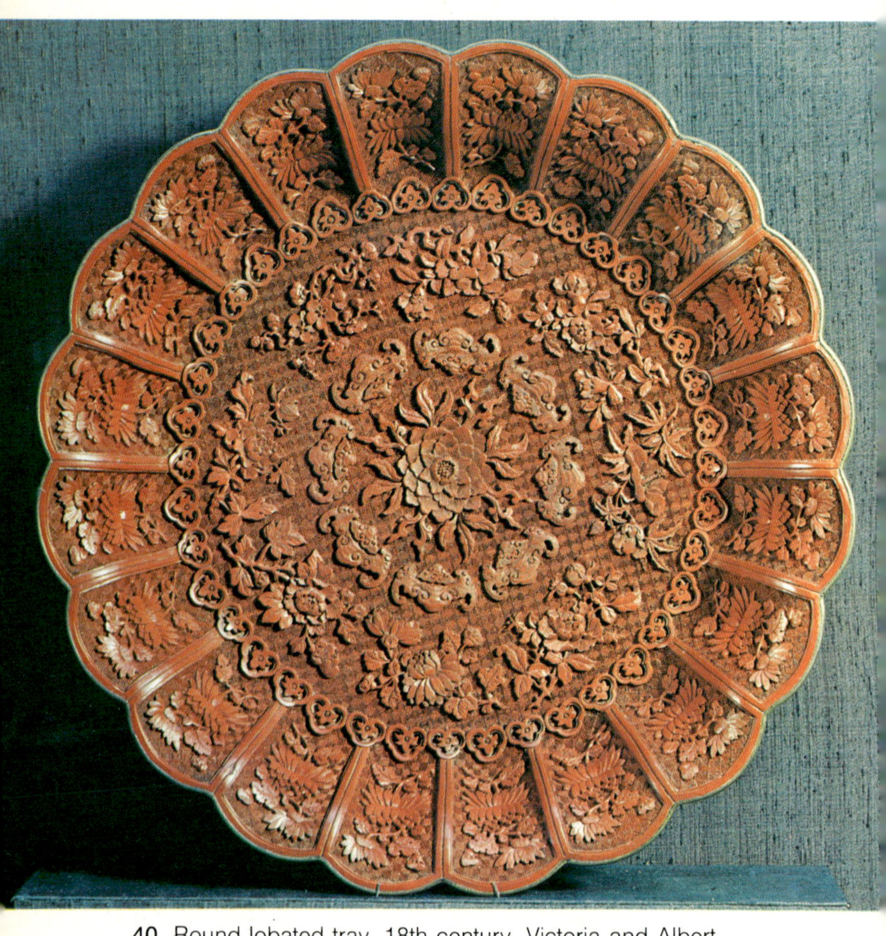

40. Round lobated tray. 18th century. Victoria and Albert Museum, London. Photo: John Webb.

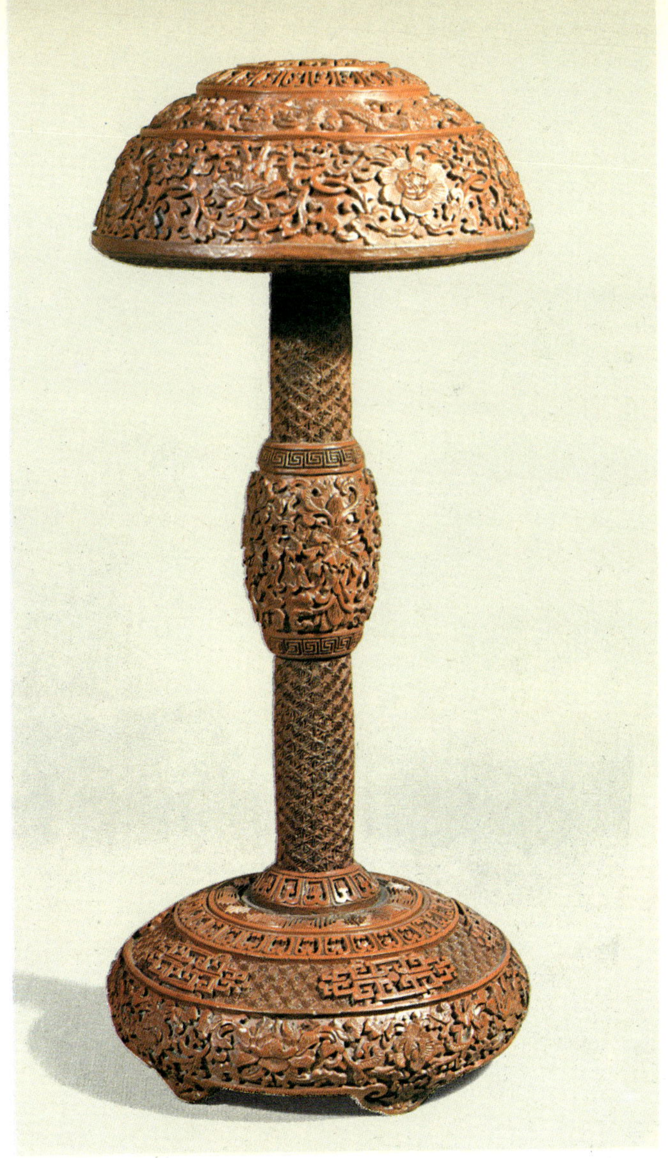

41. Cap-stand. 18th century. British Museum, London. Photo: John Webb.

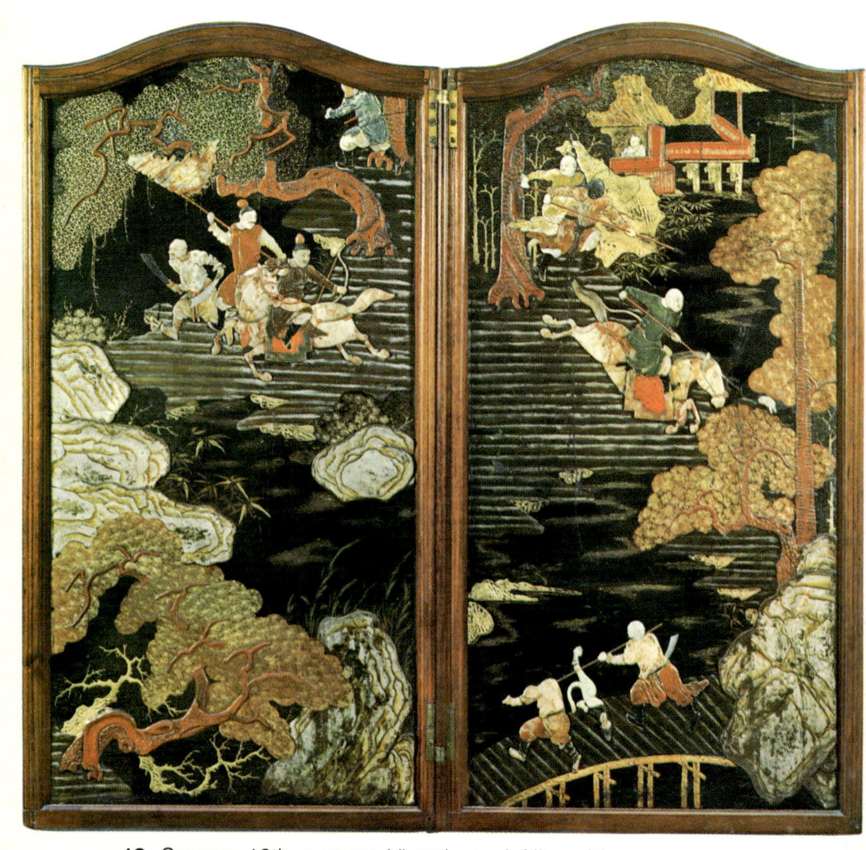

42. Screen. 18th century. Victoria and Albert Museum, London. Photo: John Webb.

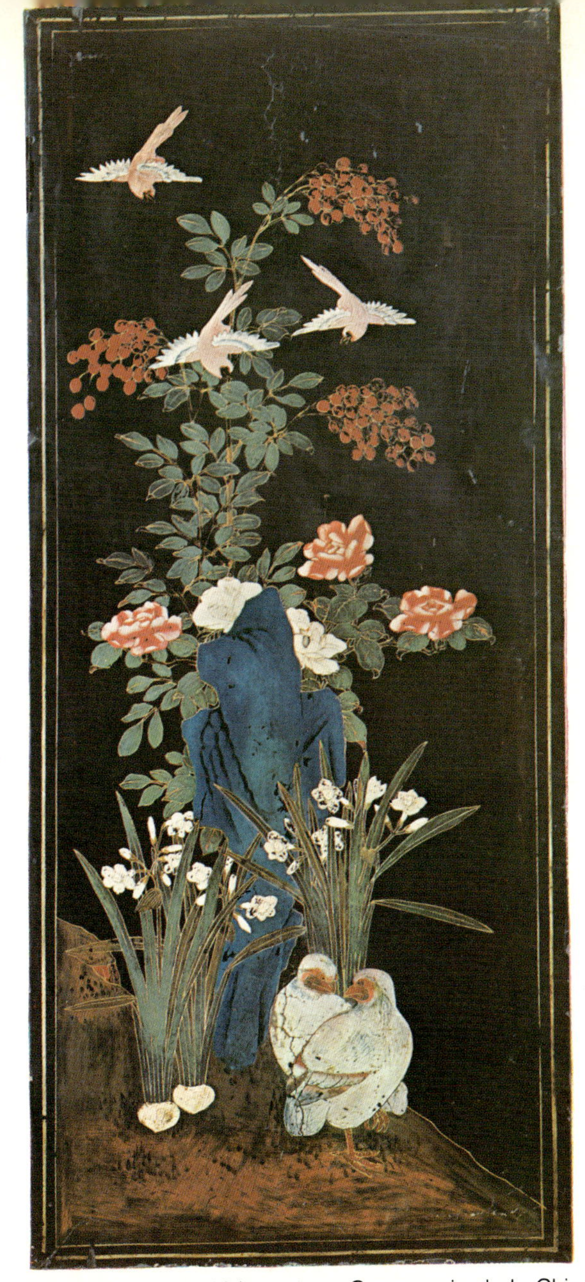

43. Leaf of a screen. 18th century. Compagnie de la Chine et des Indes, Paris.

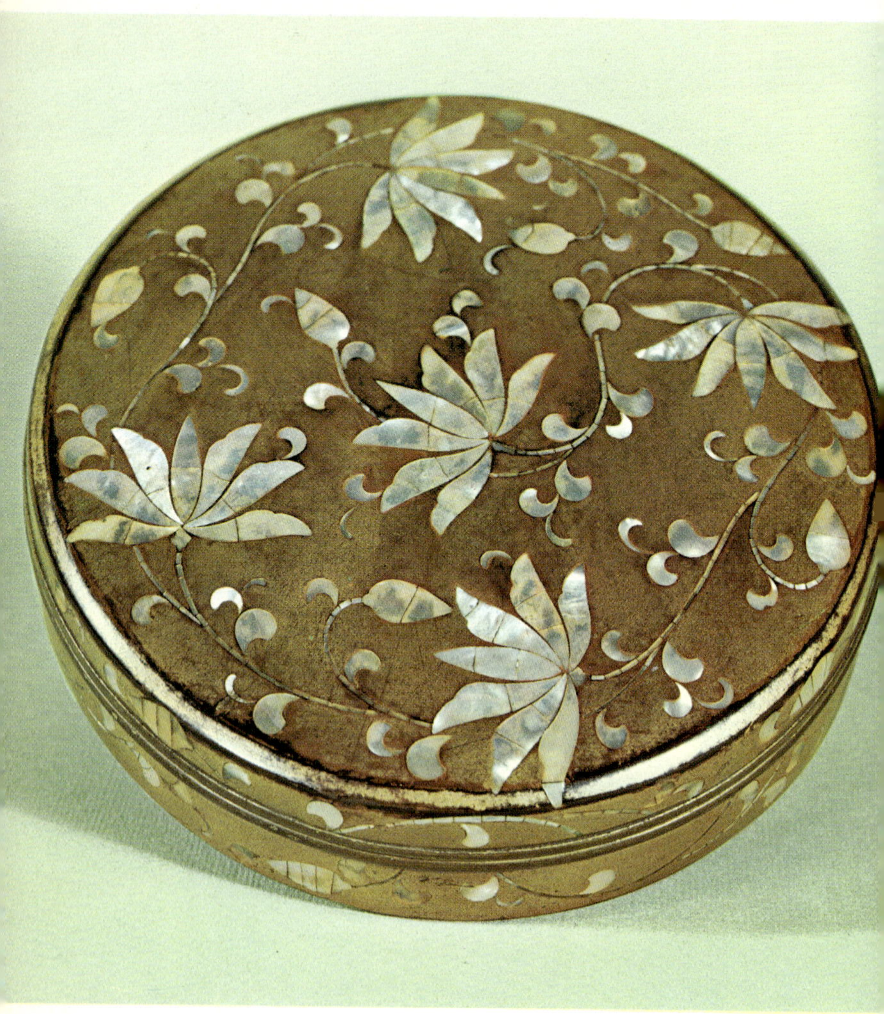

44. Round box for cosmetics. 18th century. Musée Guimet, Paris.

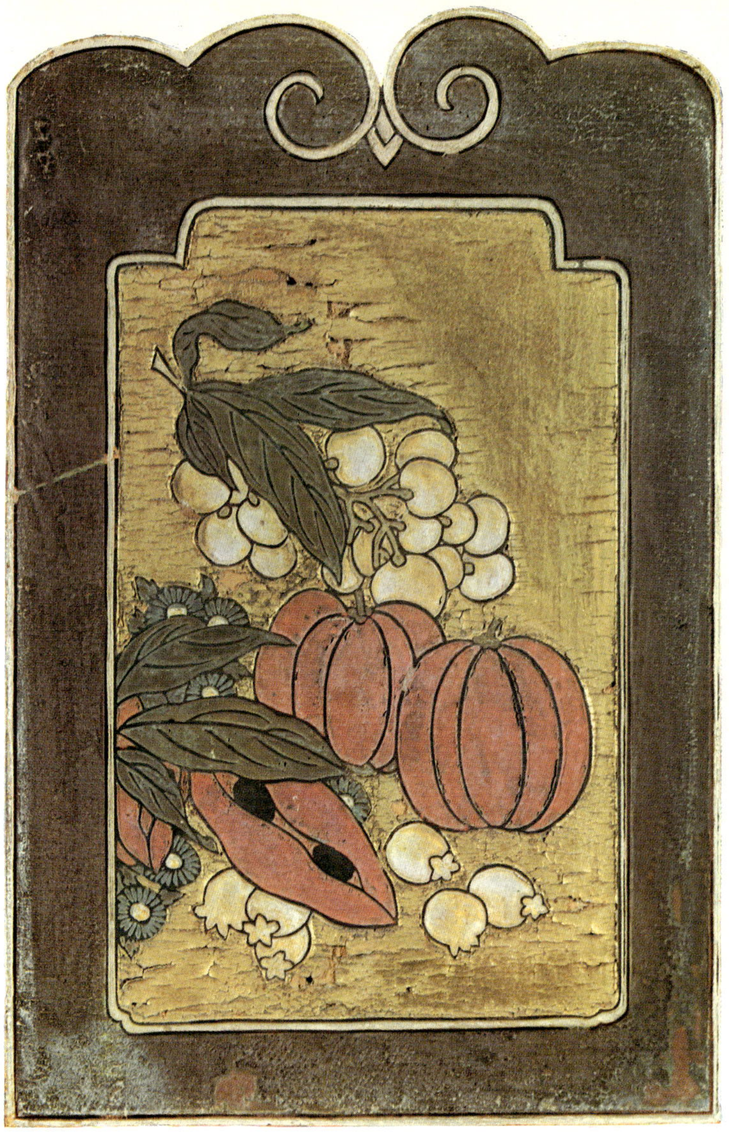

45. Small screen. End of the 17th century. Compagnie de la Chine et des Indes, Paris.

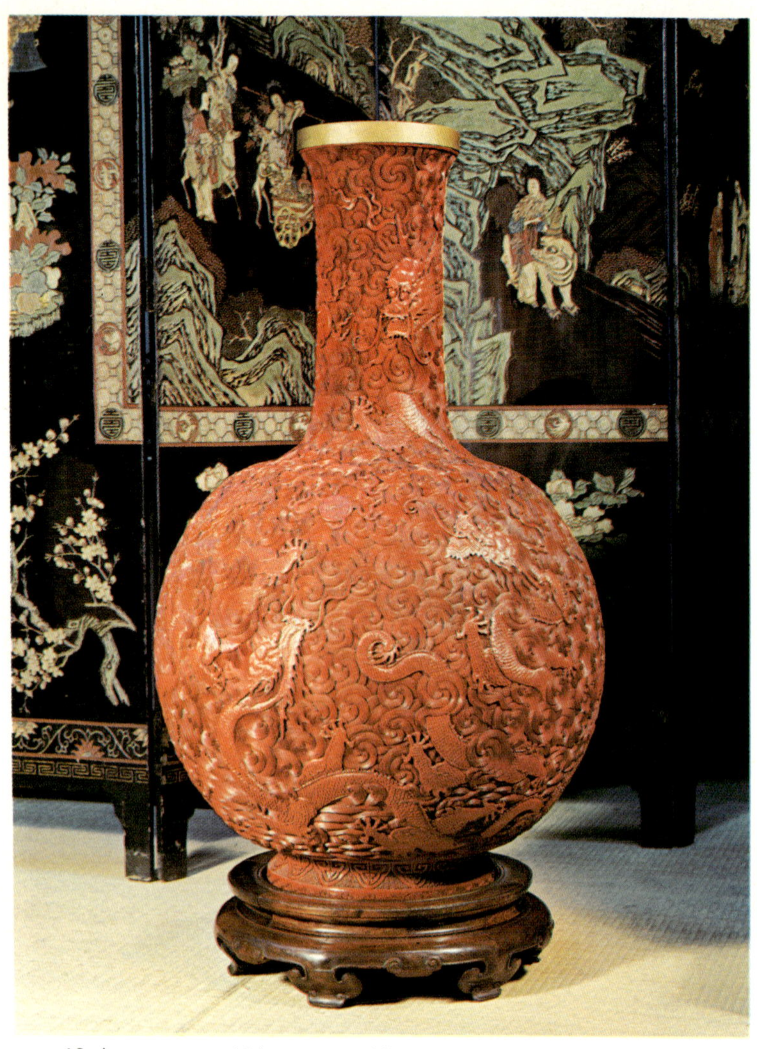

46. Large vase. 18th century. Victoria and Albert Museum, London. Photo: John Webb.

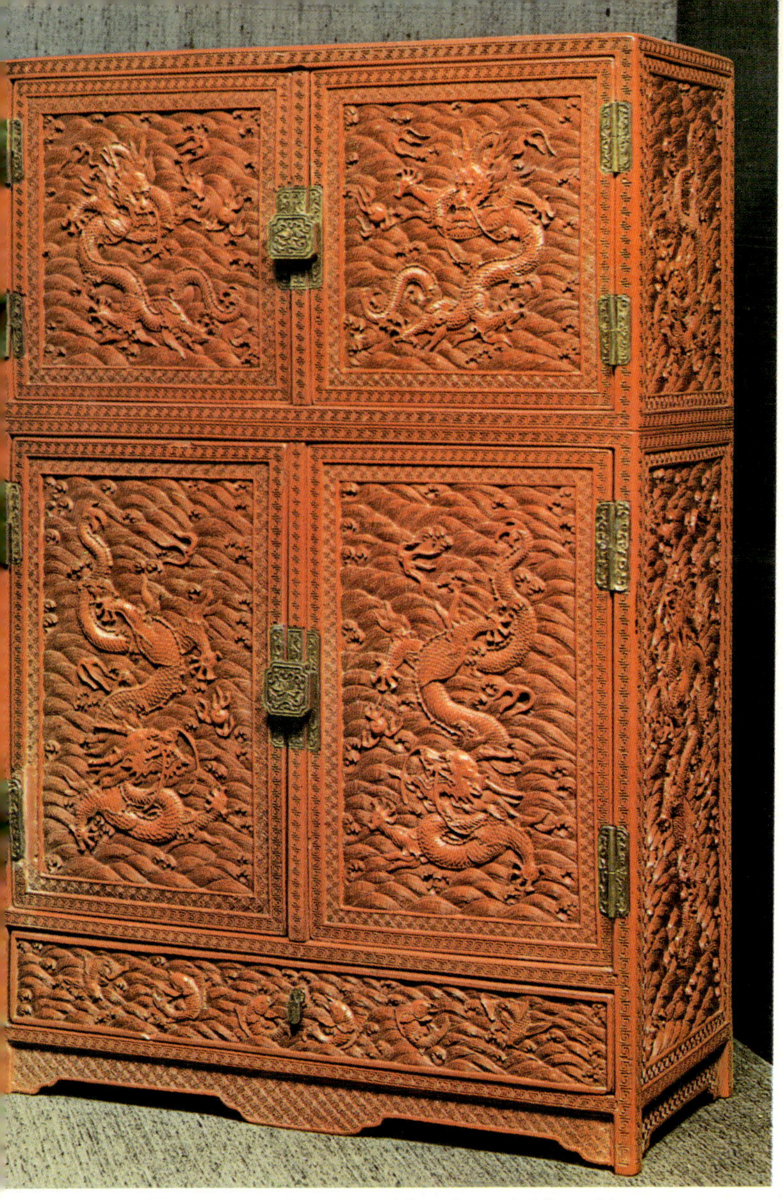

47. Wardrobe. 18th century. Victoria and Albert Museum, London. Photo: John Webb.

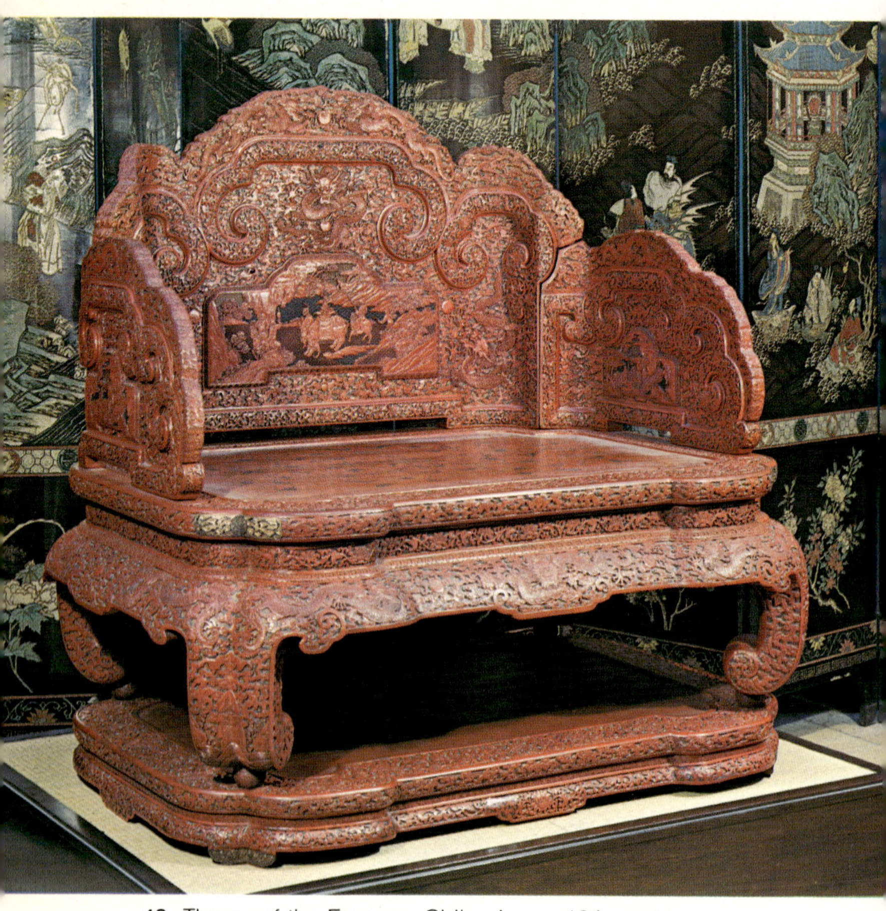

48. Throne of the Emperor Ch'ien Lung. 18th century. Victoria and Albert Museum, London. Photo: John Webb.

(usually twelve) were decorated with pictures forming a single story—figures or landscapes perhaps inspired by an ancient legend or a scene from domestic life; a great variety of subjects were used. The oldest examples, attributable to the K'ang Hsi period, are characterised by severe simplicity of treatment and incisive clarity of design; all the available space was not filled. Later, the decoration became less impressive and more elaborate and crowded. Not long ago I saw an enormous screen, part of the Collection de la Compagnie de la Chine et des Indes in Paris, that may have been painted by a Jesuit living in China in the 18th century. It portrayed the whole of the story of Christ, but the people were shown in the Chinese style of the time. The contrast between the tempera colours, delicately opaque and faded with age, and the unfaded, brilliant background of the lacquer creates an intriguing and beautiful effect, perhaps even superior to that of the original.

The Coromandel technique was also applied to panels for furniture, doors and other fittings, although these are rarer. The Emperor Ch'ien Lung, the last great Chinese sovereign (1736-1795), was particularly fond of incised red lacquer, and a very large number of works from his period have survived in China and elsewhere. Many of them bear his *nien hao* (the date expressed in terms of years since the Emperor's accession). One of his thrones, in finely incised red lacquer, is in the Victoria and Albert Museum (plate 48). Almost all the works of the Ch'ien Lung period are superb examples of craftsmanship; but the absolute precision of the technique, the over-elaborate detail and crowded design preclude all personal characteristics, so that they must be regarded as marvels of patience and virtuosity rather than works of art. From the 18th century onwards, gaudier and cheaper screens were made; jade work was very common, and discarded pieces (and other hard stones) were used to form the shapes of flowers, fruit and so on. Some specimens were of course more carefully and richly made, but generally speaking these screens cannot be regarded as works of art. In the second half of the 19th century, lacquering as an art died out completely in China, and all lacquer work has since been mass-produced.

JAPANESE LACQUERS

In the past, at any rate, the Japanese have claimed that their lacquer techniques originated independently of the Chinese; their first 'master-lacquerer' is said to have worked in the 4th century BC. As I pointed out in the first chapter, this is highly unlikely. Japanese chronicles date the beginning of the present Imperial dynasty from the year 660 BC. But even if this is accepted as historically true—and the mythical origin ascribed to the first Emperor, Gimmu Tennō, obviously brings it into question—the fact remains that the social and political unity of Japan dates only from the Yamato period (AD 100-551). The period is named after the district whose governing clan was that of the present Imperial family. It is not possible to speak of a national culture or national organisation before the 5th and 6th centuries AD; and it could be said that Japan entered history solely by way of contact with a Chinese civilisation already two thousand years old. As we have seen, this contact was made via Korea.

Japanese chronicles refer to a mythical lacquer worker, Mitsumi-no-Sukunè, who is supposed to have founded the first school of lacquering (called 'Nuribe' or 'Urushibe') towards the end of the 4th century BC. They are contradicted by another chronicle, admittedly of doubtful authenticity, which states that Prince Yamato-daki discovered lacquer by chance. The prince lived at the court of the Emperor Keiko (AD 72-130). According to this account, he was hunting in a wood one day, broke the branch of a tree and noticed that a black liquid flowed from it. (Actually, the sap or resin of the lacquer plant is milky at the time of extraction; it becomes black only after long exposure to air.) The chronicle goes on to tell how he conceived the idea of using it, decorated objects with it, and later conferred the title of Court Lacquerer on a servant who had been his assistant.

It is not difficult to account for the many legends about the origin of lacquer, which was highly thought of in Japan; and it is scarcely surprising that the powerful nationalistic spirit of the Japanese led them to claim its discovery as their own. More reliable accounts are to be found in later literary works. The *Engishiti,* which was written in 380 and survives to this day (though inevitably with alterations), mentions red and gold lacquer objects as a great novelty. Even these probably came from Korea. It is quite certain that lacquer work had begun in Japan in the period immediately before that of Nara; in other words, between AD 550 and 710.

According to a document in the Imperial archives which is believed to be authentic, the Emperor Kotoku Tennō (645-654) imposed taxes on the production of lacquer. A later monarch, Temmu Tennō (673-686), caused a kind of official department to be set up to regulate its manufacture. The same Emperor had a list of the twenty best artists made, and they were invited to affix their signatures to any works they produced. His successor, Mommu Tennō, ordered the owners of large estates to reserve a certain proportion of their land for the planting of lacquer trees. This suggests that there were originally no large natural plantations of *Rhus vernicifera* in Japan, that the tree itself may have been imported and that its cultivation was still limited.

Mommu Tennō had come to the throne in 697 at the age of fourteen; he died in 707, leaving a baby son (the future Shōmu Tennō) under the regency of the Dowager Empress, Gemmyō (707-715). It was Gemmyō who founded Nara, the first settled capital of Japan. Previously the capital had been changed when an Emperor died; possibly it was believed that a place became impure when an Emperor—who was of divine descent—had died there. Nara remained the court residence until 794, later becoming a kind of religious capital. Gemmyō abdicated in 715, leaving the throne to her daughter Genshō (715-724). It was on Genshō's orders that the first great embassy was sent to China. The head of the delegation was Kibi-no-Mabi, a great littérateur and artist. After an absence of eighteen years, he brought back sacred Buddhist texts translated into Chinese from Sanskrit, and a first-hand account of the T'ang court.

A detailed account of the journey survives. The Japanese emissaries followed the south-west coast of Korea and reached China by land, finally arriving at the capital, Changan. No doubt Kibi-no-Mabi was a very able diplomat as well as a littérateur, and had sound political motives for wishing to establish an entente between China and Japan.

The earlier hostility between the two states concerned matters of some importance to the development of lacquer in Japan. Shortly after the fall of the Western Han (AD 8), Korea was divided into three independent states: Silla, Koguryo and Paekje. Many Chinese remained in Korea, and China kept the north-western province of Liaotung as a colony. The Japanese more than once thought of occupying these three states, which were constantly at war with each other. However, Koguryo defeated a Japanese fleet which tried to invade her in the 5th century. From the outset, the T'angs had adopted a policy of prudence in their policy towards Korea, remembering the heavy losses sustained by the Japanese and by the Emperor Sui in their own attempts at conquest. But when the king of Silla sought Chinese help against a coalition of the other two states, a mighty Chinese army intervened, occupied Paekje and turned it into a Chinese colony. The king was deported to China but a *bonze* (Buddhist priest) who enjoyed great prestige started a revolt and called in the Japanese, who sent a war fleet. This was destroyed by the Chinese, and Paekje ceased to exist (663). Many Koreans fled to Japan, where they were cordially welcomed and gradually absorbed into the community. The Koreans had learnt the Chinese art of lacquering centuries before, and its exponents received considerable encouragement in

Japan, the more so because the art enjoyed the favour and interest of the Emperor. The first great lacquer artists who have passed into history as Japanese were in fact probably of Korean or Chinese origin.

To return to the ambassador Kibi-no-Mabi. He carried out his peace mission so well that the war in Paekje was forgotten. Sino-Japanese relations remained cordial throughout the T'ang period, and no fewer than fifteen Japanese embassies went to China in the period up to AD 886, when there began the protracted conflict culminating in the fall of the reigning house (906).

Those who took part in all these journeys must have brought back many *objets d'art* of great value as gifts for the Japanese Emperor. 7th-8th century lacquered objects, made in Japan but mostly the work of Chinese craftsmen, are still to be seen in the Shōsōin of the Todaiji temple at Nara, where they were placed by the Dowager Empress when Shōmu Tennō died in 756. The oldest piece of lacquer work made in Japan is the 'little temple of Tamamushi', done by order of the Emperor. It was probably executed by a Korean artist towards the end of the 7th century, and is still in good condition. It stands about six feet high, and is made of wood lacquered in black with an iridescent decoration composed of the hard outer wing-cases of beetles (the '*tamamushi*').

The lacquer has painted Buddhist figures in red, yellow and green. The colouring and design of the somewhat abstract figures are so obviously inspired by Han lacquers that the artist could not have been Japanese. In any case, if he had been Japanese, he would almost certainly have signed it, as this was apparently the custom of court artists.

A slightly later work, also in the Shōsōin, is the oldest piece which can definitely be identified as Japanese. It is the sheath of a dress-sword belonging to the Emperor Shōmu, and therefore dates from about the middle of the 8th century. The decoration is in *makkinru* style, the earliest Japanese style of decorating in gold on lacquer. The effect was obtained by covering the object with a fairly thick coating of lacquer and, while the final layer was still soft and sticky, laying on the decoration with large gold filings (not dust). The piece was later covered with another coat of lacquer; when this was dry, it was rubbed down with a very fine dust so as to leave a brilliant surface which was sufficiently transparent to allow the design underneath to show through. (This technique of rubbing down the lacquer to obtain transparency was called *tojidashi* in Japanese.) The decorative motif on this sheath is of beasts among clouds. Gold decoration had been widely used in China long before this work was made, but it must be admitted that the *makkinru* technique using large filings was a Japanese invention. It has certainly not appeared in any work found in China up to the present time.

Towards the end of the 8th century, the first statues in dry lacquer (*kanshitsu*) were made in Japan. (This, it must be remembered, simply means a lacquer without a rigid framework, not a special technique of lacquering.) The Japanese method was to make a model of the statue in crude clay which was scraped out once the lacquering was finished. There are a large number of great Buddhist statues in dry lacquer in the principal hall (*Kondo*) of the Todaiji temple at Nara. This temple was built by Ganjin at the command of Shōmu Tennō. Ganjin was not a Japanese artist, but a Chinese Buddhist monk called Chein Chên who reached Japan in 754. In all probability, the statues in the temple are the work of Chinese artisans who emigrated with him. From the 8th century, the Japanese used an innovation of their own when working in dry lacquer, covering the whole statue in gold leaf. This technique was also used, though only to a very small extent, in China.

Two groups of masks for sacred dances also date from this period. About 150 are kept in the Shōsōin, almost all of them in such a perfect state of preservation that they are still sometimes used for special ceremonies. The majority are in thin wood, but some have lacquers of different colours. They represent ancient mythological figures or demons, all rendered in a very exciting and powerful manner.

Lacquered wooden statues were apparently introduced into Japan by the Chinese, and were first of all made in one piece. Chinese sculptors had always been compelled to make statues in several pieces, because trees with tall trunks were scarce; but in Japan there was an abundance of them. These first Japanese wooden statues were of course rather compact and stocky in style, but this heightened rather than lessened their impressiveness. In the Fujiwara period (897-1185) there was a return to the Chinese method of making the statue in several parts, possibly in the interests of greater flexibility.

In 794 the capital was transferred to Heian, from which the modern city of Kyōto has developed. The Heian Era covers a span of almost four centuries, from 794 to 1185. With the economic growth of the country, there arose an aristocratic society which led a life of pomp and ceremony in the new capital. Strangely enough, it was the art of lacquer work which benefited most. It was no longer restricted to the decoration of useful or ornamental objects, but was employed to beautify the interiors of the new palaces and the finish on furniture. Furniture in Japan, however, was more limited in quantity and variety than in China; for whereas chairs, armchairs and divans had been everyday objects in China for many centuries, in Japan they had only recently been introduced.

The *makie* technique using gold-dust was the most popular, and indeed reached its peak in this period. This was because new devices had been invented which allowed the reduction of gold to a fine powder, and because the discovery of new veins of gold made the raw material available in large quantities. Another method of decoration perfected in Japan was the use of inlaid mother-of-pearl (*raden* in Japanese), a typical example of a technique taken over from the Chinese. The oldest existing work of the Heian period is a book-case (*sasshi-bako*) with a basic decoration of flowers and leaves: it is now in a temple at Kyōto. Research suggests that it may have been made for the Emperor Kuammu (782-805); and according to the tradition of the temple which houses it, it was used to hold the Buddhist *Sutra* for the *bonze*, Kobo Daishi, in the first half of the 9th century. Another view, favoured by most modern experts, is that it was donated to the temple in 1919 by the Emperor Daigo. The use of a base of *makkinru* for the decoration—a technique almost wholly abandoned by the second half of the 9th century—leads me to believe that it may be older. Its decoration includes a picture of the mythical bird which lives among the honeysuckle in the Celestial Spheres.

From the 10th century there are more reliable

accounts. These come from the Imperial Archives, since the art of lacquering was considered a matter of national importance. A new method of lacquering, using incrustations of mother-of-pearl, is mentioned at some length in the book *Mogaturi,* written in about the middle of the 10th century by the famous woman writer Murasaki Shikibu. The Emperor Kuazan (984-986) reigned for only two years. (He abdicated after the death of his favourite concubine, and became a *bonze.*) Kuazan took a personal interest in the making of lacquer, and ordered the court lacquerers to protect the edges of lacquered objects by placing a thin band of metal around them. A similar method of preventing wear and tear was adopted in Sung China for the fragile porcelain Ting Yao cups.

The second half of the Heian Era is known as the Fujiwara period (897-1185), after the powerful family which in effect controlled the Emperors. There was intense competition between the nobles and the Emperors, who tried to outdo one another in the construction of grand, ornate Buddhist temples. Almost all of these had sumptuous lacquered interiors, and many still exist. In the temple of Byodoin, on the outskirts of Kyōto, the principal room is called the Amida room because of the great statue of that Bodhisattva in it; all its wall are decorated in *raden* style. The temple was originally a residential palace, built by one of the Fujiwaras in the first half of the

11th century. The interior of the temple of Chusongi, built by another Fujiwara in 1126, is decorated in black lacquer and gold leaf.

The Fujiwara period is a watershed in the history of Japanese art, which ceased to be copied from China and developed specifically Japanese characteristics. In 988 the Emperor Ichijio sent the Chinese Emperor T'ai Tsung some gold-lacquered works which had been made by his court craftsmen. On the face of it, this was sending coals to Newcastle; in fact the gifts were much appreciated, and as a result Japanese techniques influenced Chinese work.

Towards the end of the Fujiwara period, a method was applied to gold lacquering which is at first sight the most obvious, namely using a flat and uniform background *(hira-makie)*. But it became a practical possibility only when the Japanese succeeded—by means of skilfully contrived tools and repeated refining—in obtaining an extremely fine form of powdered gold. *Hira-makie* had to be made with complete accuracy because the slightest defect was very noticeable on a surface that was bare, smooth and shiny.

In 1185, after fighting had taken place between the two most powerful clans, Yoritomo, the supreme head of the victorious faction, organised his own military government with its seat at Kamakura. From that time there were two governments and two capitals in Japan: one at Heian (Kyōto), which was the residence of an almost powerless Emperor, and the other at Kamakura, which was the seat of the effective government and the Shogun. (This title corresponds roughly to the Western 'generalissimo'.)

During the whole of the Kamakura period (1184-1333), art received no great encouragement. The firm discipline imposed on the military by the Shogun obliged them to live rather austere lives, while the Imperial court lived under the shadow of the military, and survived only because of the Emperor's supposedly divine origin. There is, however, a very beautiful writing-desk which dates from the beginning of the period. It is in gold lacquer decorated with chrysanthemums and birds with inlaid mother-of-pearl. It is kept in the temple of Tsurugaoka at Kamakura, and is said to have been given to the first Shogun, Yoritomo, by the Emperor in 1195. Incised lacquer had not yet come into use, but there was some innovation at this time: the *kama-kura-bori* technique, which consisted of incising the decoration on the object before lacquering took place, and the *taka-makie* or relief design obtained by using lacquer upon lacquer. This method, which allowed more freedom of style and a more varied and original type of composition, received a new impetus in the next period, the Ashikaga (1333-1568). To make the decoration stand out in greater relief, very fine ochre was mixed with the pure lacquer, in no way detracting from its durability and beauty. Famous painters of the Tosa school devoted themselves to the art of lacquer, creating many masterpieces, and Japanese gold lacquer was of such excellence that its fame spread overseas. In about 1430 the Emperor Hsuan Tê sent some of his court lacquerers to Japan to learn new techniques.

From the Ashikaga period the subjects used for decoration became more varied: not only conventionalised figures, birds and flowers, but temples, landscapes and scenes. They were portrayed with an eye for detail, and with rare harmony and sense of balance. All the known techniques were used, including a new one which consisted of inserting into the lacquer tiny fragments clipped from sheets of gold or silver (*kiri-kane*). In the 15th century, the Japanese art of gold lacquer crossed into China, while the fashion for incised red lacquer travelled in the opposite direction. In the Imperial capital, a great lacquerer named Monyiu perfected the technique of making oblique incisions into alternate layers of red and black lacquer, cutting fine black lines which completed the elegance of the decoration.

In 14th-century Japan, the Nō theatre, somewhat similar to that of the Greeks, was created. In order to make an immediate impact on the eye, the actors used masks which, though almost always tragic or menacing, often contained a certain ambiguity of expression —a hidden amusement or irony. The Nō theatre later gave rise to another theatrical form, the 'Kioghen', which may be described as a short farce. Nō masks sometimes reveal a remote Chinese influence, but the comic Kioghen mask may well be considered an original art-form. Such masks must not be thought of as portraits: they represented types, not individuals. Many of them are lacquered, some carrying the signature of a famous artist on the inside (especially in the Ashikaga period); they are unquestionably works of art in their own right.

There were many important lacquer artists in the brief Momoyama period (1568-1600). One favoured technique was to create a smooth gold background and then put a relief decoration in gold on it (usually chrysanthemums or other flowers); it was finished with an overlay of mother-of-pearl or clippings of silver. At about the end of this period, a certain Koyetsu became very famous. He was born at Kyōto and went to the Tosa school of painting. After he left, he decided to devote himself to lacquer work. He achieved admirable results, integrating all known styles and techniques into his work, and introducing a new technique of his own. This was to lay thin sheets of lead, clipped into the shapes of tiny flowers, animals or rocks, on to smooth gold or shining black surfaces; the lead figures stood out from their luminous backgrounds with astonishing effect. As lead is soft and easily marked, the already described *tojidashi*

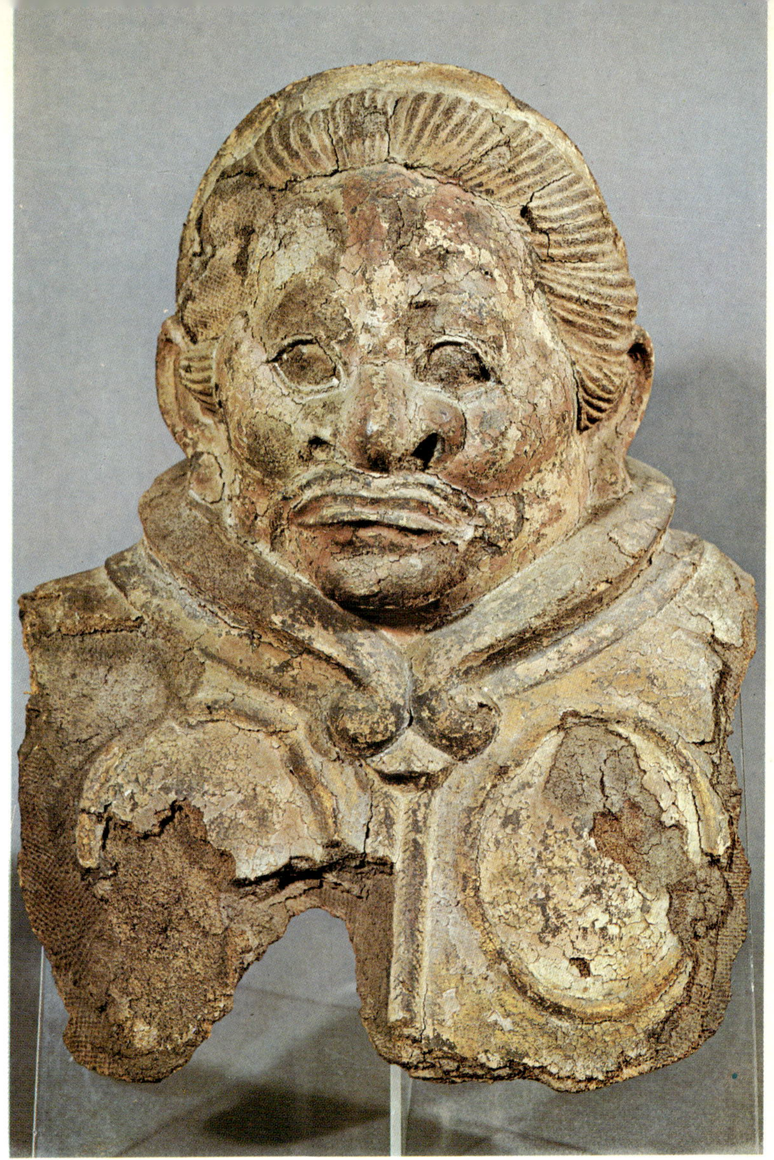

49. Statue in dry lacquer. 8th-9th century. Musée Guimet, Paris.

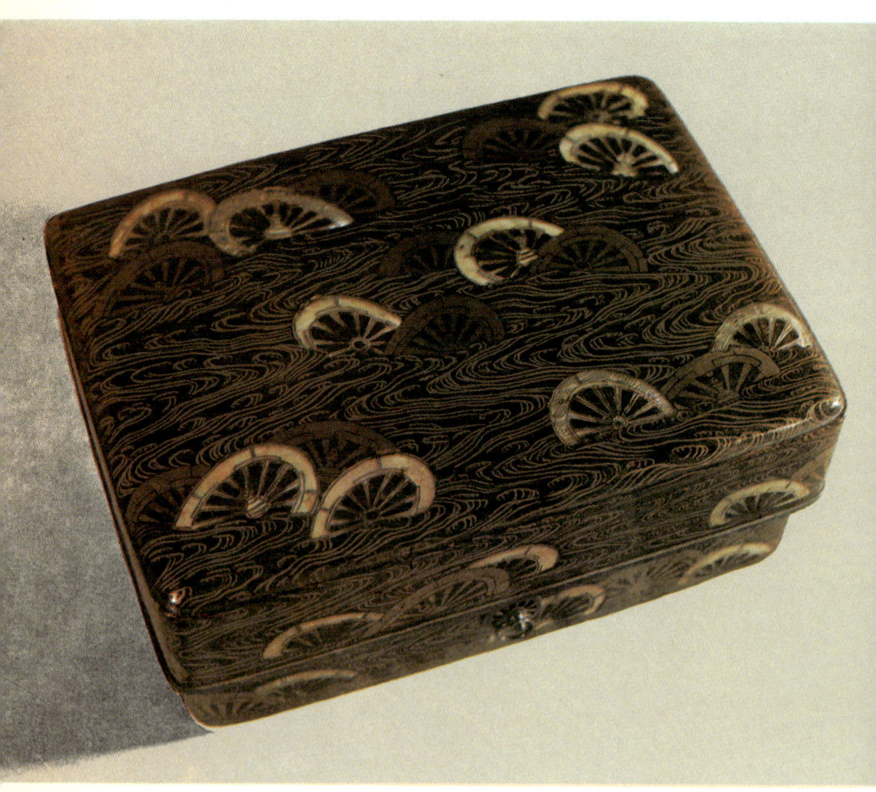

50. Small rectangular box for cosmetics. 8th-12th century. National Museum, Tokyo.

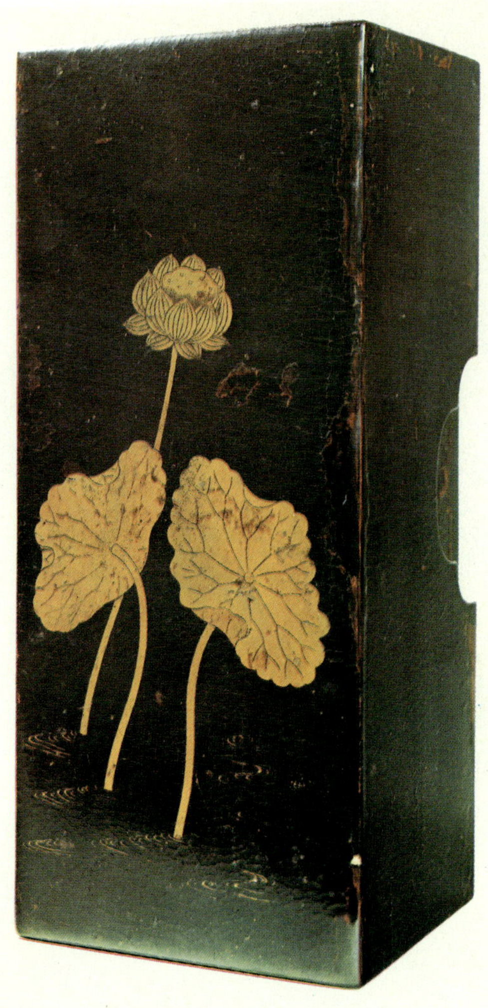

51. Rectangular box. 12th-14th century. Musée Guimet, Paris. Ex Koechlin Collection.

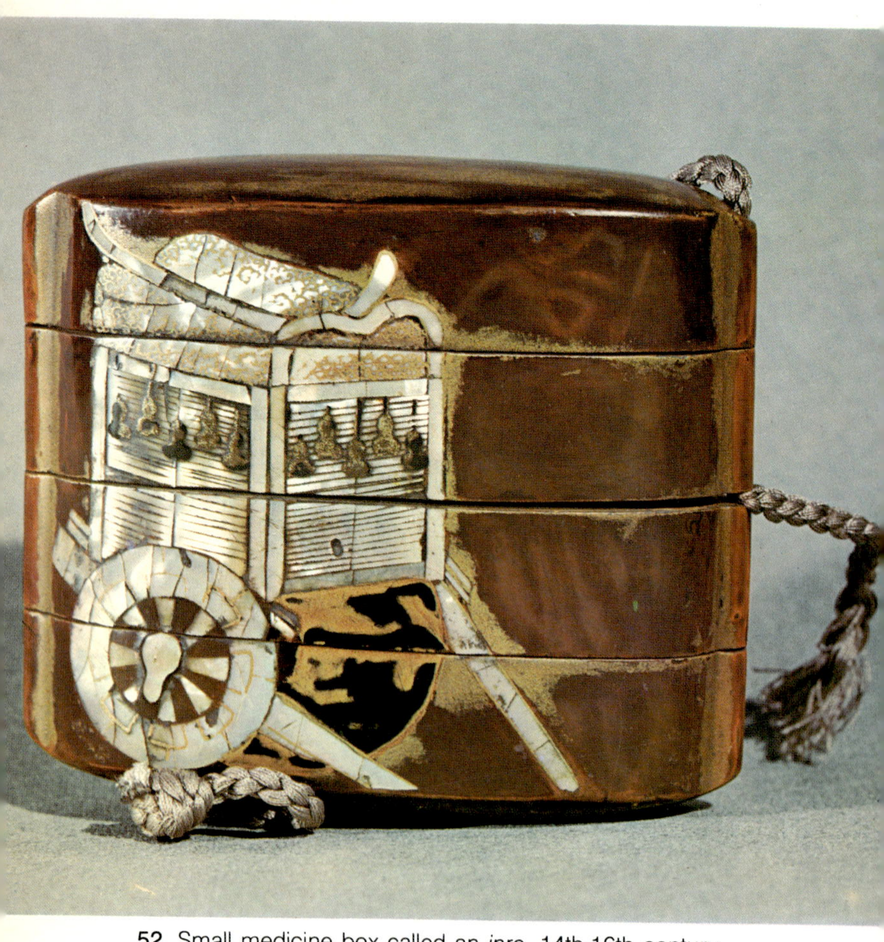

52. Small medicine box called an *inro*. 14th-16th century. Compagnie de la Chine et des Indes, Paris.

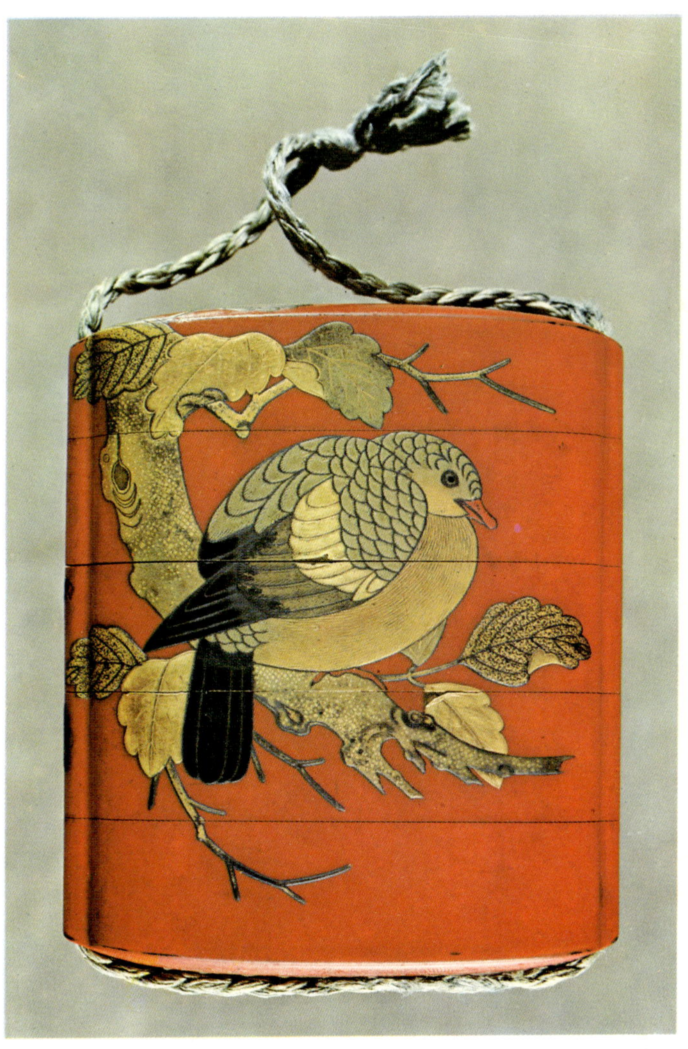

53. *Inro*. 17th century. Museo Orientale, Venice.

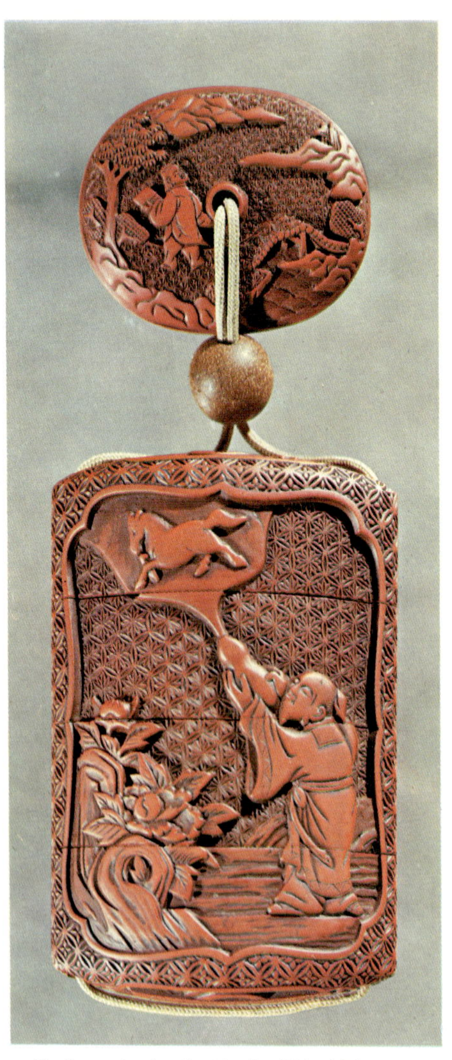

54. *Inro*, with its *netzuke* (button). 17th-19th century. Museo Orientale, Venice.

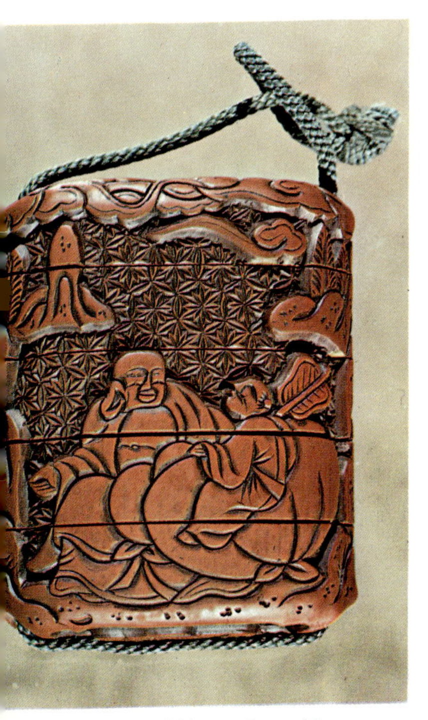

55. *Inro.* 17th century. Museo Orientale, Venice.

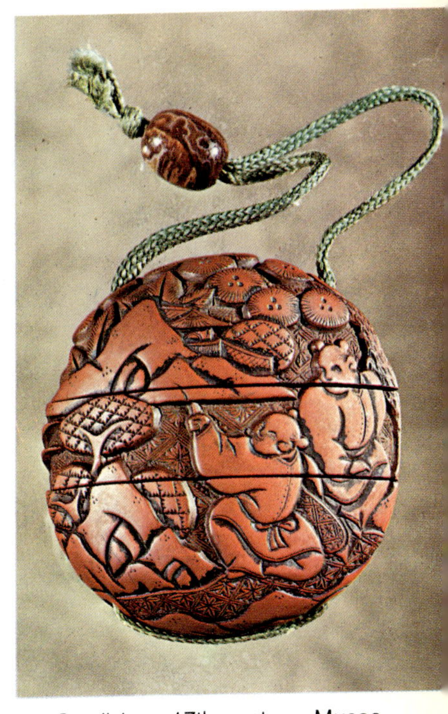

56. Small *inro.* 17th century. Museo Orientale, Venice.

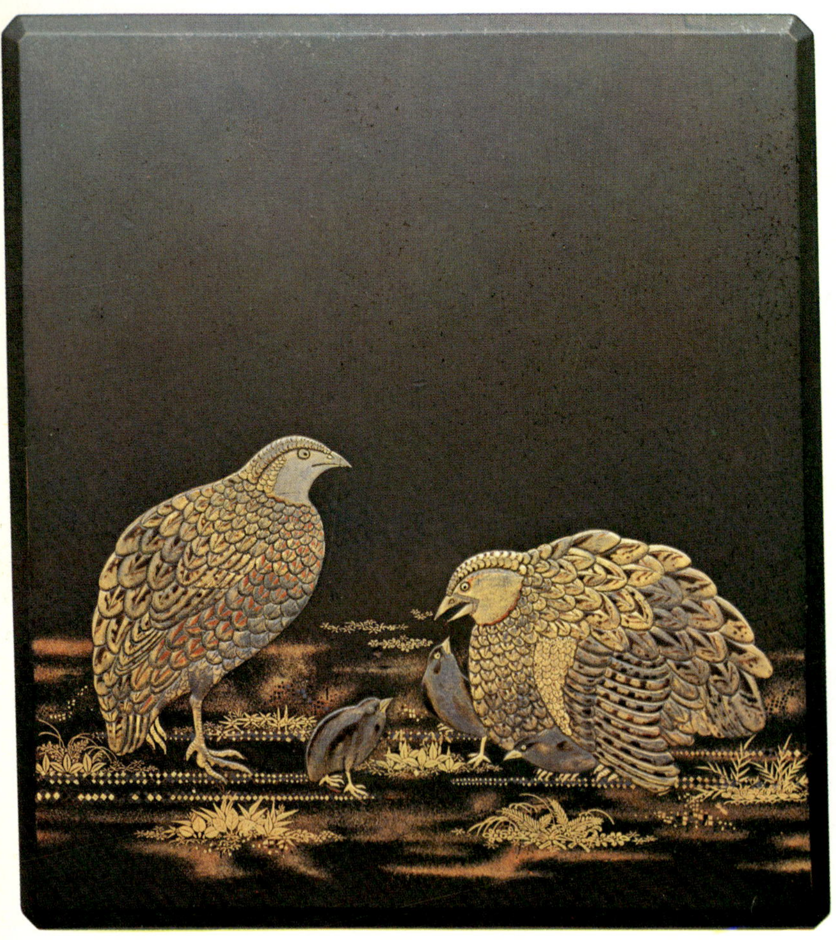

57. Box for writing materials. 17th century. Museo Orientale, Venice.

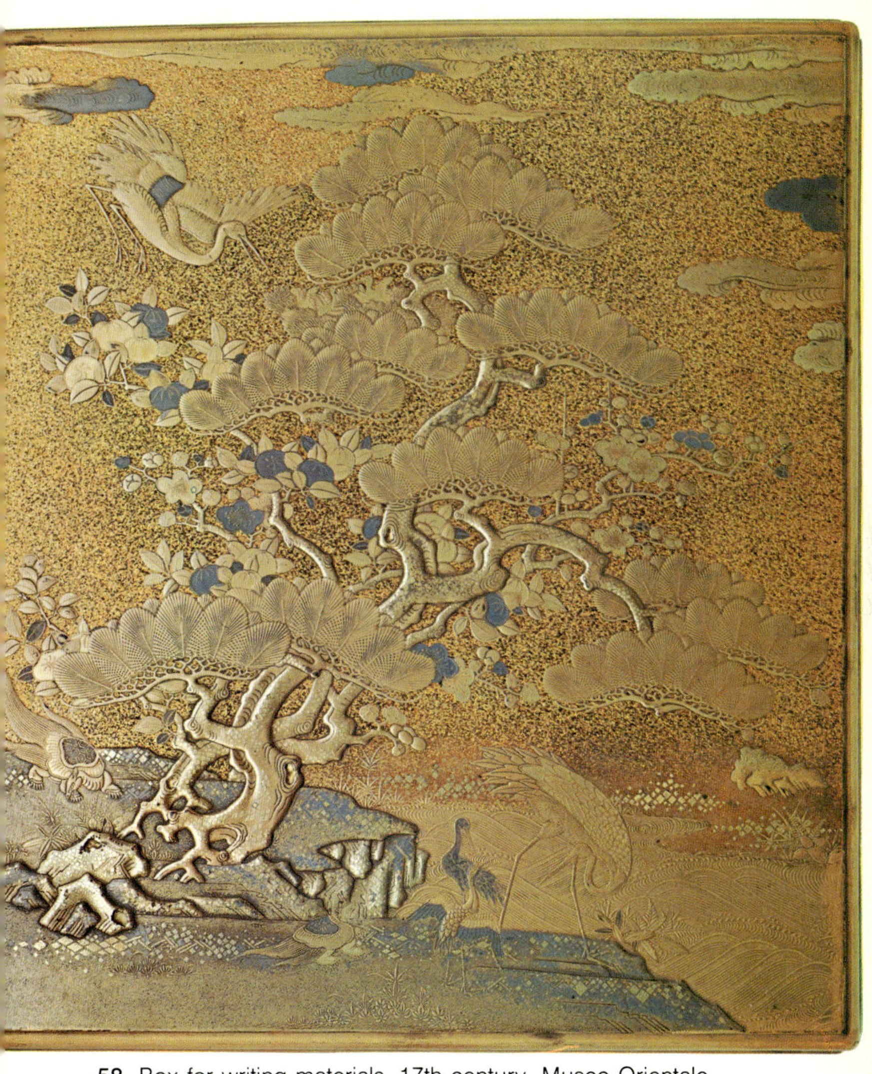

58. Box for writing materials. 17th century. Museo Orientale, Venice.

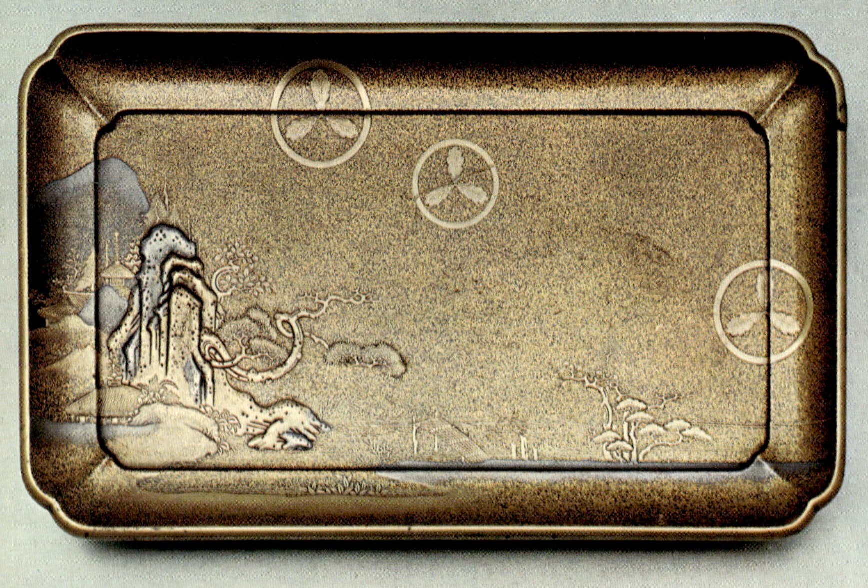

59. Rectangular tray. 18th-19th century. Museo Orientale, Venice.

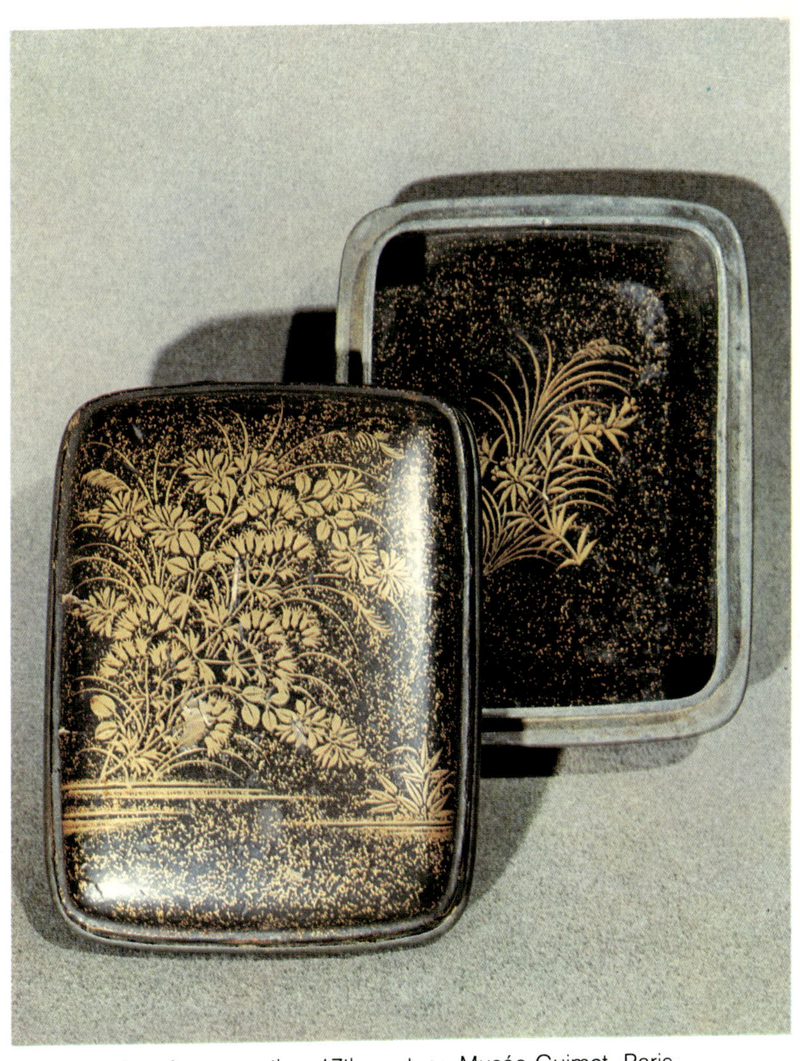

60. Box for cosmetics. 17th century. Musée Guimet, Paris.

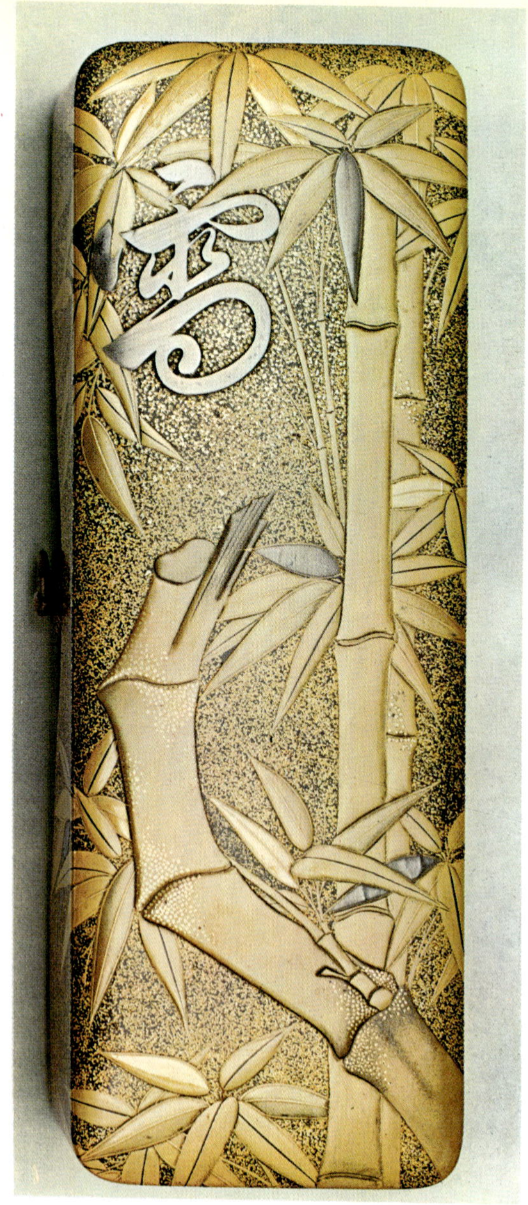

61. Box for writing materials. 17th-19th century. Museo Orientale, Venice.

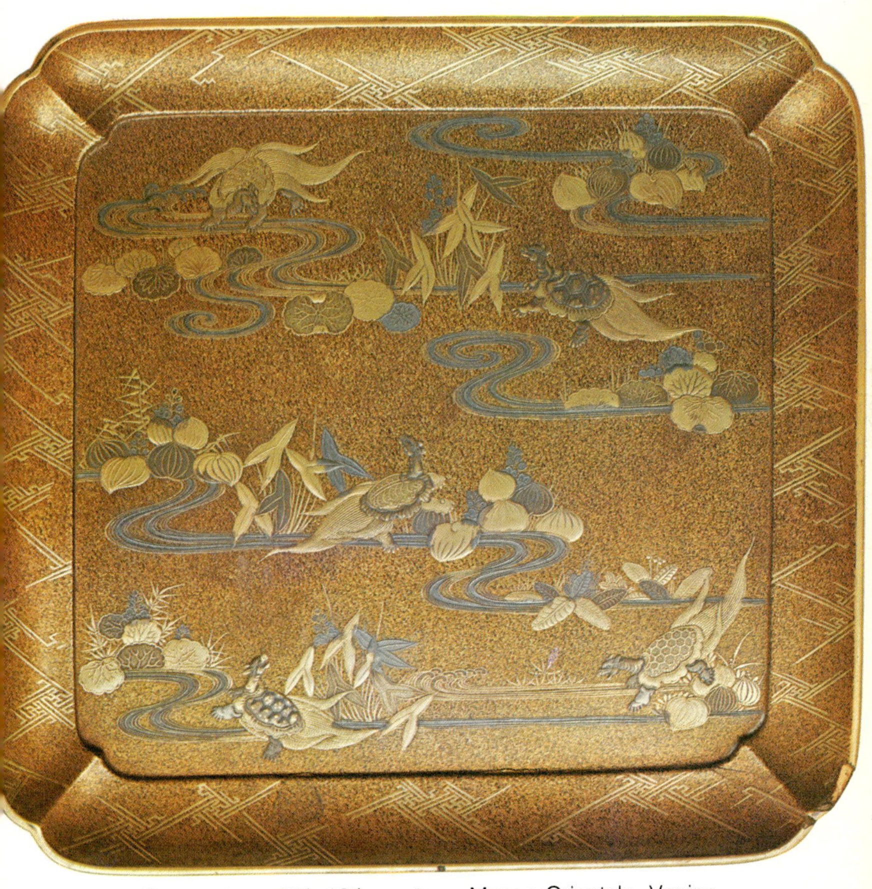

62. Square tray. 17th-19th century. Museo Orientale, Venice.

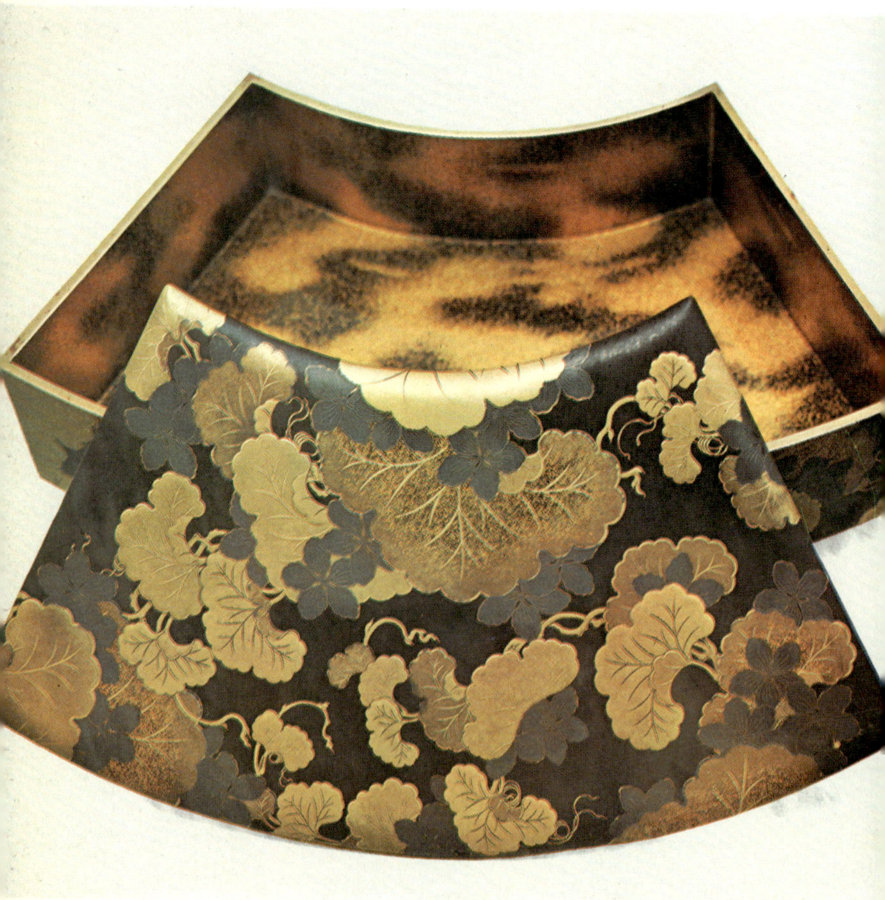

63. Fan-shaped box. End of the 18th or beginning of the 19th century. Museo Orientale, Venice.

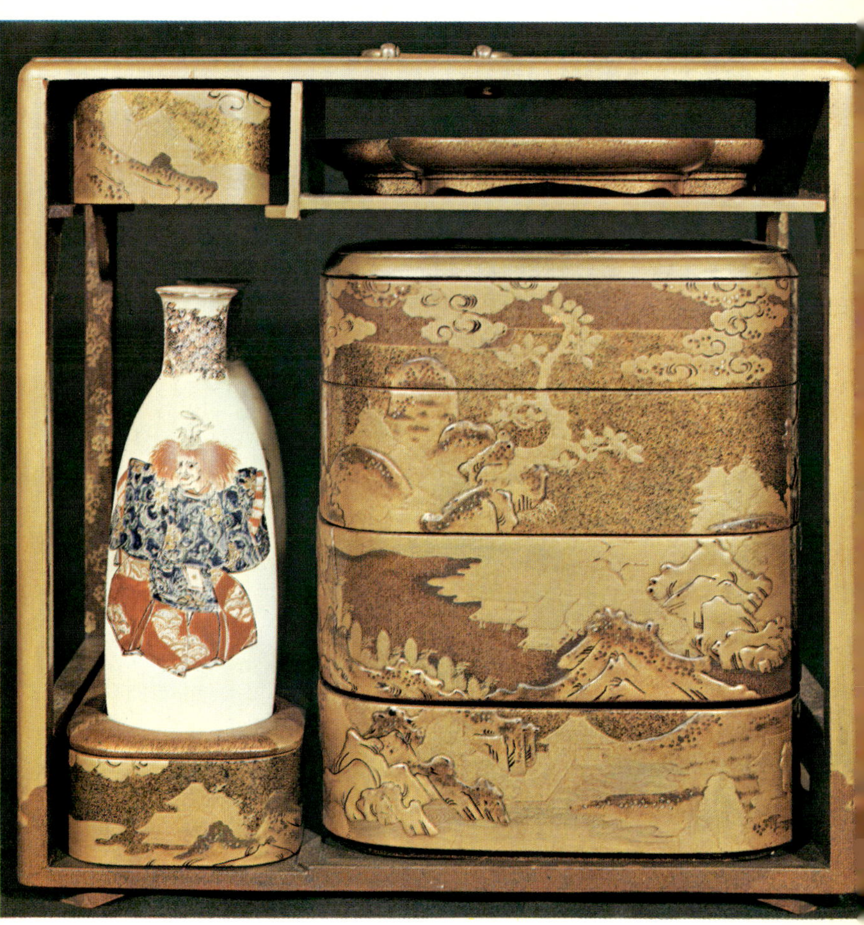

64. Set of utensils for a light meal. 19th century. Museo Orientale, Venice.

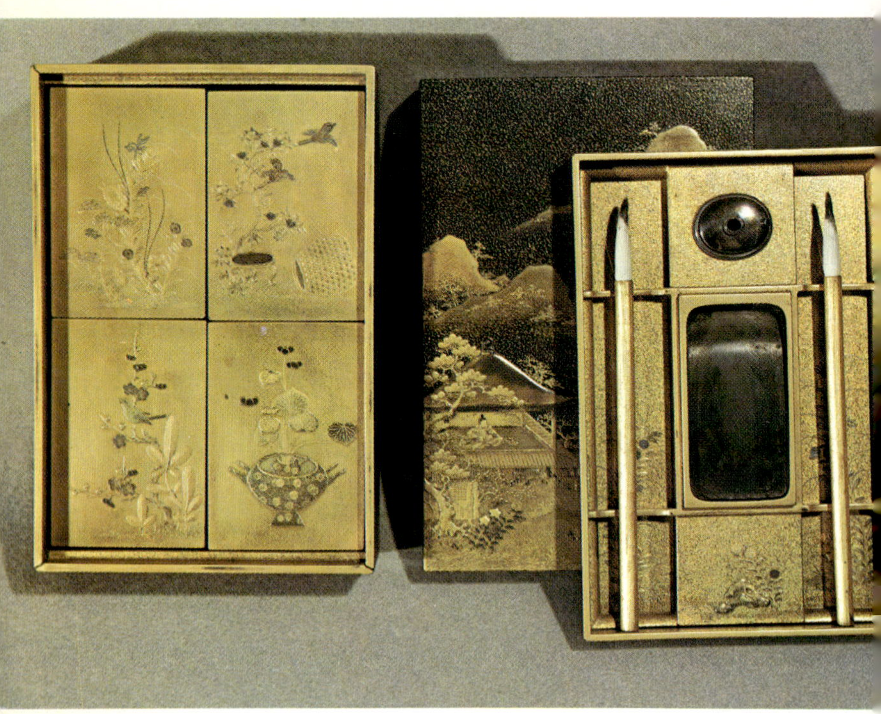

65. Set of writing materials. 18th century. Musée Guimet, Paris.

technique was of course applied: after the metal pieces had been inserted, the surface was levelled with more lacquer and the whole piece given a final coat of lacquer with a brush; later, when it was dry, it was rubbed down.

The Edo or Tokugawa period lasted until 1867, when the long period of feudal military rule ended and the Shogunate ceased to exist. During the period the finest Japanese lacquer work of all was produced. The background decoration continued to be gold, as in *makie* or *hira-makie,* but great painters competed to create masterpieces of an elegance and variety of style which have never been surpassed. The Shoguns of the Tokugawa family abandoned the Spartan simplicity of the first Shogun and maintained courts whose pomp and splendour rivalled or even surpassed that of the Emperor. About halfway through this last period of military government, Japan passed through a period of peace and prosperity which favoured the growth of a new class of rich merchants, who sought to vie with the nobles in display. This was a further stimulus to the manufacture of lacquered goods. Lacquering was an almost obligatory part of the decoration of interiors, of furniture, sets of tables and writing-desks; and it also served to beautify two objects which had become indispensable to every citizen with any pretensions to wealth: a little box for medicines *(inro)* and one for tobacco, which were attached to the belt by a cord. No artist, however famous, thought it beneath him to decorate an *inro*.

Easily the greatest artist of the Edo period was the versatile and brilliant painter Ogata Kōrin (1658-1716). Kōrin fell completely under the spell of lacquer work, and finally dedicated himself to it entirely. He adapted his inventive and powerful style of painting to making objects in *makie*, achieving new and original effects. (His brother Kenzan was incidentally one of the greatest Japanese ceramic artists.) His lacquer work is characterised by an intense vibrancy and less definition than is usual in Japanese work. It is difficult to describe: the slightly opaque and perfectly even surfaces, as if made of a massy block of gold, seem to emanate power and warmth. Using the most diverse materials—silver, lead, tin—to obtain different tones of grey, he succeeded in fusing and blending them against a gold background, obtaining a depth of perspective never achieved by any other artist.

Kōrin lacquers are very rare because they were enthusiastically collected by his rich contemporaries; but there is one splendid example in the Berlin Museum. Kōrin also collaborated with his brother in the decoration of ceramic works, and there is a rectangular tray with vivid azure irises, bearing the mark of Kenzan and the signature of Kōrin, in the Metropolitan Museum.

Ritsuō (1663-1747), a pupil of Kōrin's, although

almost the same age, survived his master by some thirty years. He continued Kōrin's work, introducing minor innovations of his own. Besides being a painter and sculptor, he was also a ceramic artist, and he liked to use fragments of his ceramic work as overlays on his lacquer works. His technique is referred to in contemporary texts as *hiaku-ko-kan,* 'incrustation with a hundred precious things'. His art was much admired, although he never reached the heights attained by his master.

Only a few 19th-century artists are worthy of mention: Koma Koryo, Izuka Toyo, Nishimura Zopiko and one or two others. Their art already displays the conventional gaudiness of 20th-century lacquer, and it was sold and exported in large quantities. Cheap, mass-produced porcelain replaced lacquer work for tableware almost completely, even in Japan; and of course the *inro*, the *netzuki*, the small receptacles for tobacco and the other tiny and sophisticated gadgets have disappeared from the daily lives of a now completely westernised people.

LIST OF ILLUSTRATIONS

1. Decorative object. 4th-3rd century BC. J. H. Wade Fund, Cleveland Museum of Art, Cleveland. Represents two strange stylised birds on a base formed by two intertwined serpents. Thinly painted on hard wood in red and black lacquer with some touches of yellow. There have been various conjectures as to the meaning of this famous work, which was found at Ch'ang Sha in Hunan province; the one most widely accepted is that it symbolises the struggle between heavenly forces and harmful, infernal ones. This is questionable, since the snake has never been a frightening symbol in China.

2. Oval dish. 4th-3rd century BC. British Museum, London. Lacquered in cinnabar red on a wooden framework. The decoration is on a black lacquer background and is similar to the metal inlays of the Chinese bronzes dating from the 'Warring States' period.

3. Round box for powder or rouge. 1st century AD. British Museum, London. Dry lacquer on frameless hempen cloth with silver inlays. The outside decoration of the box has curved ornamental motifs enclosing a symmetrical and horizontal arrangement of a dozen or so small figures representing symbolic animals and a strange feathered man. On the lid there is a large quatrefoil in silver, and the outer rim has a band portraying a hunting scene with mounted archers made in silver overlays.

4. Oval dish with side flanges. 4th-3rd century BC. British Museum, London. Lacquered in red on a wooden framework. The decoration is of semi-geometric curves on black lacquer, in a design which recalls those of metal inlays on the bronzes of the 'Warring States' period. From Ch'ang Sha (Hunan).

5. Oval bowl with two flanged handles. 1st century BC. British Museum, London. The decoration, which is in lacquer upon lacquer, consists of whorls and stylised birds painted in red and yellow on a black background which has faded. The bowl is of particular value because it carries an inscription giving the exact date of its manufacture, a list of the people concerned in its production, and the name of the Imperial overseer employed to supervise the work.

6. Decorative antefix. 3rd-6th century. Musée Guimet, Paris. Probably an antefix in hard wood, lacquered in brown. It may represent a later evolution of the classical T'ao-t'ieh monster. Six Dynasties period.

7. Bowl in the shape of a lotus flower. 10th-13th century. Musée Guimet, Paris. Monochrome lacquering on a wooden framework. Its simplicity calls to mind the classic forms of Sung ceramics (it belongs to the same period).

8. Large wooden statue. 12th-13th century. Private collection, Milan. Polychrome lacquer on very fine sheepskin over a wooden framework. It represents a Kuan Yin in the position of 'regal repose'. From Shensi, Chin period.

9. Statue in gold lacquer. 14th century. Private collection, Milan. This is made on a plaster frame. It represents an upright Kuan Yin. The statue is some 27½ inches high and probably belongs to the end of the Yuan period or the beginning of the following Ming period.

10. Box for sweetmeats. 18th-19th century. Musée Guimet, Paris. The box is made up of a number of compartments in black lacquer, inlaid with mother-of-pearl garlands of flowers. Yuan period, or the beginning of the Ming period.

11. Box. 15th century. Musée Guimet, Paris. This box is in cinnabar lacquer with a clearly carved floral design. It probably dates from the Hsuan Tê period.

12. Cosmetic box. 18th century. Compagnie de la Chine et des Indes, Paris. This five-lobed box is in cinnabar red on a metal frame. Overlays of mother-of-pearl for petals and tiny pieces of green jade for leaves are used in the complex floral decoration of the lid. In the centre is a large camellia in mother-of-pearl. The rim of the lid has a narrow band of silver lightly engraved in continuous Greek fret design (*lei wen*).

13. Round box for rouge. 16th century. Victoria and Albert Museum, London. Photo: John Webb. Yellow, black and red dry lacquer. Coats of black lacquer have been laid on top of many layers of yellow lacquer; the red was used for the final touches. Taoist emblems are hidden in the bold floral decoration, while on the lid Lao Tse is portrayed surrounded by his Eight Immortals. The figures, rocks and peripheral ring of the lid have some gold lacquering which has partly worn away.

14. Lacquered metal bowl. 16th century. British Museum, London. Photo: John Webb. Metal bowl with very thick red lacquering. The vigorous carving which leaves great empty spaces is an indication of antiquity. The rather rounded edges of the carving suggest a dating around the second half of the 16th century, probably the Chia Ching period.

15. Vessel with lid. 16th-17th century. British Museum, London. Photo: John Webb. Closely carved and incised cinnabar lacquer. The shape is reminiscent of the censers of the late Ming period, usually ceramic. The crowded decoration indicates the beginning of a decline in the art: the personality of the artist is being lost in mere technical virtuosity. Wan Li period.

16. Travelling box. 16th-17th century. Musée Guimet, Paris. Background of coral lacquer highlighted in gold. The decoration includes groups of two dragons, one in cinnabar lacquer and the other in black. A ring in the middle (symbolic of the fiery pearl of purity) contains the character Shou (long life). Wan Li period.

17. Lobated box. 2nd half of the 16th century. Fernanda Sona Collection, Milan. Carved and incised red lacquer on a wooden framework. The central figures are vigorously carved and there are large unfilled spaces. This is typical of older works; from the 17th century the decoration was more crowded.

18. Cabinet with two doors. 16th century. Compagnie de la Chine et des Indes, Paris. Finely incised and painted coral lacquer. The decoration, which has been executed with great skill, shows the front of a palace giving on to a garden where children are playing under the eyes of their two governesses. Ming period.

19. Red lacquered coffer. 17th century. Compagnie de la Chine et des Indes, Paris. This coffer has a wooden frame and is richly decorated in polychrome lacquer. The two large erect dragons facing each other in the central motif clearly have four claws on their feet. This object was therefore not intended for the Emperor's use; whenever the dragon was used as a decorative motif on objects for the court, it had to have five distinct claws. Late Ming period.

20. Lacquered wood casket. 16th-17th century. British Museum, London. Photo: John Webb. Small casket in wood with thick cinnabar lacquering; the surfaces are deeply carved and clearly incised. Wan Li period.

21. Polychrome lacquer tray. 16th century. British Museum, London. Photo: John Webb. The sides of the tray are deeply incised and the contrast of colour is obtained by the superimposition of two layers of lacquer of different shades. The centre of the tray was painted afterwards with blue lacquer and geometric designs in gold, which has partly worn away. The background is of flowers painted in yellow lacquer and the decoration of the sides is a repeated one of good-luck symbols, including the character Shou (long life) and the figure of a bat.

22. Tray. 16th-17th century. Cornelia Blakemore Warner Fund, Cleveland Museum of Art, Cleveland. Tray in red and black lacquer; worked like a *cloisonné,* the lacquered areas being separated by silver wires. The decoration includes animal, vegetable and mineral motifs. This quite sophisticated work belongs to the Wan Li period.

23. Cabinet with several compartments. 16th century. Norman O. Stone and Ella A. Stone Memorial Fund, Cleveland Museum of Art, Cleveland. Finely carved cinnabar lacquer on wood. The sole decorative motif is a series of five-clawed dragons surrounded by clouds; hence this object was probably intended for Palace use. It belongs to the Ming period and bears an inscription dating it in the twenty-second year of Wan Li.

24. Wine jug. 16th-17th century. Victoria and Albert Museum, London. Photo: John Webb. The decoration of the spout, handle and outside rim of the neck is made with flakes of powdered gold, blown on in a way which was more common in Japan. The decoration of the body of the vessel is in polychrome lacquer with encrusted mother-of-pearl. The shape is typical of similar ceramic articles of the Wan Li period.

25. Double container. 16th-17th century. British Museum, London. Photo: John Webb. A double container shaped like certain types of pumpkin; in carved cinnabar lacquer on a metal framework. At the centre are two large Chinese characters, 'Great' and 'Good Luck'. Wan Li period.

26. Rectangular box. 16th-17th century. Musée Guimet, Paris. Large box in incised cinnabar lacquer on a wooden framework. The scene is of a summer pavilion in a grove, with some human figures. The rather close-packed decoration indicates the beginning of a decline in this art-form, which was at its height in China in the 15th century.

27. Hexagonal casket with lid. 17th century. Victoria and Albert Museum, London. Photo: John Webb. Red lacquer with lateral decoration of flowers and leaves. The dome-shaped lid is divided into six scenes showing children at play, a theme regarded as symbolising good fortune.

28. Round box for sweetmeats or cosmetics. 17th century. Zlata Kovacevic Collection, Milan. Wooden framework which, in view of the depth of the carved figures, must have received at least 250 coats of cinnabar lacquer. Although the style suggests that this work is older (perhaps 15th-century), the lateral decoration of uniform and inexpressive characters and the rounded cut of the central scene prove that it is of later date.

29. Lobated box for cosmetics. 17th century. British Museum, London. Photo: John Webb. On the borders, the lacquer is a coral colour and finely incised; on the lid the decorative effect is achieved by placing two layers of lacquer, one black and one red, one on top of the other.

30. Round bowl with lid. 17th century. British Museum, London. Photo: John Webb. Cinnabar lacquer deeply incised on both the body and the lid. The decoration consists of the character Shou (long life) repeated four times; the bowl was probably an anniversary gift. The shape is reminiscent of that of a tea dish.

31. Censer. 17th century. British Museum, London. Photo: John Webb. Cinnabar lacquer on a metal framework. Protruding from the lid is a knob which is perhaps meant to represent the traditional Chinese fruit, *lee chi.*

32. Vase. 18th century. Compagnie de la Chine et des Indes, Paris. Vase in cinnabar lacquer, deeply and richly carved; it must have received more than 250 coats of lacquer. Four central medallions, symmetrically spaced around the body, portray people and foreshortened views of palaces; the rest of the crowded decoration is floral. Ch'ien Lung.

33. Rectangular tray. 17th century. Victoria and Albert Museum, London. Photo: John Webb. Carved cinnabar lacquer on a wooden frame. In spite of the accurate execution and a certain depth of carving in the central part, the crowded decoration denotes the beginning of a decline. This work probably belongs to the last twenty years of the reign of Wan Li.

34. Screen in Coromandel lacquer. 17th-18th century. Compagnie de la Chine et des Indes, Paris. The scene is of a maiden leaning towards a young man, perhaps to offer him a flower, while a servant-girl stands at her shoulder looking on. The decoration on the sides is restrained. A work of very high quality, belonging to the K'ang Hsi period.

35. Screen in Coromandel lacquer. 17th-18th century. Compagnie de la Chine et des Indes, Paris. The slight fading which has taken place over the years has lent an even more delicate tone to the polychrome decoration. The scene shows an important personage, followed by one of his servants, walking through a peaceful and pleasant landscape. The border is decorated with highly stylised dragons. A delicately-made work of excellent quality. K'ang Hsi period.

36. Black lacquer wardrobe. 18th century. Musée Guimet, Paris. Large Imperial wardrobe painted with gold lacquer on a black lacquer background. The somewhat over-abundant decoration consists exclusively of dragons which are pursuing the 'sacred pearl of purity'. In a circle at the bottom is the customary good-luck character Shou. Late K'ang Hsi period.

37. Black lacquer wardrobe. 17th-18th century. Musée Guimet, Paris. Large Imperial wardrobe finely decorated in gold lacquer on black lacquer with mother-of-pearl inlays. On the front panels are two landscapes; on the base is the Imperial symbol of two five-clawed dragons pursuing the sacred pearl. K'ang Hsi period.

38. Detail of a screen. 17th century. Compagnie de la Chine et des Indes, Paris. Red Coromandel lacquer with gold lacquer medallions representing flowers, animals (including a stork) and human figures in a variety of attitudes.

39. Lacquered wardrobe. 18th century. Victoria and Albert Museum, London. Photo: John Webb. Wardrobe lacquered entirely in black and decorated with pictures made in coloured and gilded lacquer. This work also has inlays of mother-of-pearl and semi-precious stones.

40. Round lobated tray. 18th century. Victoria and Albert Museum, London. Photo: John Webb. Cinnabar lacquer on a wooden frame. Superb floral decoration on at least 200 coats of lacquer. The pattern is dense and elaborate.

41. Cap-stand. 18th century. British Museum, London. Photo: John Webb. This strange object is richly incised in red lacquer on a wooden framework. Ch'ien Lung period.

42. Screen. 18th century. Victoria and Albert Museum, London. Photo: John Webb. Lacquered in black; it has a lively polychrome decoration of coloured lacquers. The effect is enhanced by overlays of thin sheets of mother-of-pearl and hard stones, and by the use of finely powdered gold dust. Ch'ien Lung period.

43. Leaf of a screen. 18th century. Compagnie de la Chine et des Indes, Paris. Leaf of a screen in black lacquer on wood. The decoration, painted in sparkling and brilliant colours, represents a rose bush and two pheasants. Touches of gold lacquer highlight this scene, which emerges vividly against the shiny black background.

44. Round box for cosmetics. 18th century. Musée Guimet, Paris. This box is in brown lacquer on a wooden framework, and is embellished with inlaid mother-of-pearl forming an intricate decoration of elegant floral motifs.

45. Small screen. End of the 17th century. Compagnie de la Chine et des Indes, Paris. Coromandel lacquer decorated with polychrome fruit on a gold background.

46. Large vase. 18th century. Victoria and Albert Museum, London. Photo: John Webb. Large vase lacquered in red on a metal framework. The extremely detailed incised decoration shows nine dragons pursuing the pearl of purity (one of the Imperial symbols). It comes from the Summer Palace at Peking and was probably removed about the end of 1900. Ch'ien Lung period.

47. Wardrobe. 18th century. Victoria and Albert Museum, London. Photo: John Webb. Wardrobe in incised cinnabar lacquer. Clear-cut decoration of dragons surrounded by clouds. Probably part of the furnishings of the Palace at Peking. Ch'ien Lung period.

48. Throne of the Emperor Ch'ien Lung. 18th century. Victoria and Albert Museum, London. Photo: John Webb. Engraved red lacquer. The very rich decoration is the main feature of this work, which was taken from the Summer Palace.

49. Statue in dry lacquer. 8th-9th century. Musée Guimet, Paris. Statue of a Buddhist monk. The gold lacquer which must originally have covered the whole statue is now quite worn. Japanese art of the Nara or Heian period.

50. Small rectangular box for cosmetics. 8th-12th century. National Museum, Tokyo. Lacquer on a wooden framework. *Raden* technique on *ro-iro-nuri*; that is, with thin flakes of mother-of-pearl, shaped like small fans, stuck into the black lacquer while it was still soft and sticky; when it was dry, the whole thing was covered with another coat of transparent lacquer. Heian period.

51. Rectangular box. 12th-14th century. Musée Guimet, Paris. Box in black lacquer on a wooden framework; intended to hold the *Sutra,* or sacred Buddhist texts. The decoration, made by inlaying thin sheets of mother-of-pearl cut in a design of a flower and two leaves, is of impeccable simplicity and power. It must have been the work of a great master lacquerer of the Kamakura period.

52. Small medicine box called an *inro.* 14th-16th century. Compagnie de la Chine et des Indes, Paris. The unusual decoration—a travelling carriage—is made of thin sheets of mother-of-pearl overlaid on a simple brown lacquer background which has been partly discoloured by time and the effect of light. *Raden* technique. Ashikaga period.

53. *Inro.* 17th century. Museo Orientale, Venice. Vermilion lacquer on a wooden framework. Decorated in gold lacquer with a sparrow sitting on a branch; overlays of thin sheets of silver and lead have been used to finish it, giving a natural effect. The work of a great artist.

54. *Inro,* with its *netzuke* (button). 17th-19th century. Museo Orientale, Venice. Deeply incised cinnabar lacquer (*tsuishu*). The scene illustrates an ancient Chinese Taoist legend which passed into Japan: an Immortal possessed a magic bottle from which he could make a fairy horse appear. Tokugawa period.

55. *Inro*. 17th century. Museo Orientale, Venice. Framework of carved wood covered with incised red lacquer (*kamakura-bori*). It shows a Lohan with his disciple.

56. Small *inro*. 17th century. Museo Orientale, Venice. This small *inro* is in the shape of the Buddhist pearl, with a button (*netzuke*) by which to hang it from the girdle. Incised cinnabar lacquer with a decoration of youths at play.

57. Box for writing materials. 17th century. Museo Orientale, Venice. Black lacquer on a wooden framework. Magnificent decoration of a pair of quail with two chicks; made by using gold lacquer and inlaid lead and tin, highlighted in red.

58. Box for writing materials. 17th century. Museo Orientale, Venice. Gold lacquer sprayed with very fine dust. The beautiful decoration is of a leafy tree growing on the bank of a river. The trunk is in high relief, while the leaves are only slightly raised from the surface and finely incised. A pleasing contrast is provided by the other metals used for the flowers and fruit. The elegance of the work is completed by the herons in very low relief.

59. Rectangular tray..18th-19th century. Museo Orientale, Venice. Wooden framework. The basic lacquer is *ikakeji* and the landscape decoration is vividly created by using lead under lacquer. Perhaps the work of Yogusai, the master of the *makie* technique.

60. Box for cosmetics. 17th century. Musée Guimet, Paris. Box lacquered in black, probably on a pewter framework. The internal and external decoration is in plain gold lacquer on sprayed *ikakeji* gold lacquer, and the design is floral.

61. Box for writing materials. 17th-19th century. Museo Orientale, Venice. Wooden framework with a lacquer known as 'aventurine'; that is, with fine gold-dust sprayed on while the lacquer is still sticky. The design of canes and leaves of bamboo displays great mastery. To obtain a more striking effect, some of the leaves are highlighted by means of fine sheet silver—the *Heidatsu* technique. A rather precious and sophisticated piece of work. Tokugawa period.

62. Square tray. 17th-19th century. Museo Orientale, Venice. The framework is of wood, and filigree silver is used to create waves or clouds in which turtles swim or fly. Tokugawa period.

63. Fan-shaped box. End of the 18th or beginning of the 19th century. Museo Orientale, Venice. Black lacquer on hard wood. The floral decoration of the lid is made with flaked or blown-gold lacquer. The technique is perfect but the design is somewhat mannered.

64. Set of utensils for a light meal. 19th century. Museo Orientale, Venice. Two porcelain bottles for rice wine, small trays, and compartments to hold salted seeds and other titbits, form a cabinet in thin lacquered wood. The designs carefully executed but somewhat stereotyped.

65. Set of writing materials. 18th century. Musée Guimet, Paris. This set in gold lacquer has been executed with various techniques; the work is enhanced by the use of metal overlays.